PAL ....

TAROT
de Marseille

Prologue by
JEAN PAULHAN
Exposé
EUGENE CASLANT

Translation into English by
Marius Høgnesen

Original French title: Le Tarot de Marseille

Year of publication: 1949 by ARTS ET METIERS GRAPHIQUES

Author: Paul Marteau

This book is an English translation of the original book in French.

Tarot card illustrations in this book are a reproduction of the Nicolas Conver Tarot de Marseille from 1760 by Emrik & Binger and printed by De La Rue in the mid to late 19th century. These cards are almost identical to the Ancien Tarot de Marseille by Grimaud, which illustrated the original book, but because of copy right issues have not been used for this book.

Images in the book have been retouched and have been subjected to minor modifications and repair.

The image used for the book cover, is a modified image from the translator´s own French edition.

First printed in March 2021. Second print October 2021.

Published by:
https://www.circleandtriangle.com

ISBN: 978-82-692706-0-0 Paperback
ISBN: 978-82-692706-6-2 Paperback (in black & white)
ISBN: 978-82-692706-1-7 eBook

INDEX

Translator's Note

As a collector of Tarot books and decks for several years, I have long awaited an English translation to surface of Paul Marteau's momentous book from 1949; *Le Tarot de Marseille*. A spark of hope was ignited a few years back, when rumour had it, a private translation was in the works, but alas to no avail, fizzling out into something about Grimaud copy right issues..

So, what was one to do? Well, here was one novel idea, I suppose I could give it a go. I mean, I had a Spanish and just recently a French copy on the shelf and I suppose could find a Tarot similar to that of the Ancien Tarot de Marseille by Grimaud (If that indeed was the card stock Marteau had in mind, when writing this book). Why not, right? But hold on! What makes a Norwegian with English as a third language, Spanish as a fourth and French borderlining the ridiculous, think he can translate this momentous book by Paul Marteau? Well, we have saying in this part of the world; "Necessity teaches the naked woman to spin," and no, this is not meant to be interpreted in any derogative way, merely that: Need facilitates produce.

The real tragedy is this; despite of this book having been around since 1949, it has never been translated into English. This is a foundational book to be sure, certainly within the Tarot de Marseille world, something akin to Arthur Waite's *The Pictorial Key to the Tarot* for the Rider-Waite community. The book is not perfect, but what Marteau did do, was set the trajectory on the reading style, we see today in Marseille Tarots.

So, I have spent around 6 months translating this important book, going line by line, paragraph by paragraph, page by page. I have done everything myself from translating to image editing, in order to get this book to a finished print ready state. The title of this book? Well, *The Tarot of* Marseille just did not sound right and *Le* would imply a book in French, so...

I do not for a moment purport to say, that this is a perfect English translation of this book, but I do contend to say, it is a fair one. No doubt some will point out my errors of translation, as the saying goes; no good deed goes unpunished. I suspect, others will do a better job of it in the future, however in the meantime, you can read this one.

I hope you will enjoy this book, as much as I have. Happy reading or as the French would have it; *Bonne lecture.*

Marius Høgnesen

In memory, of
EUGENE CASLANT

PROLOGUE

CONCERNING THE GOOD USE OF THE TAROT

On the nature of the Tarot, some understand rather little and others too much. Scholars sometimes see in them a perpetual almanac, a forecasting and sometimes a course in morals, on metaphysics, on alchemy, a game, the simple fantasies of a playing card maker, an occult pact or a gift. Their comments, both gratuitous and hostile, finally provoke a genuine desire not to speak of Tarot in more profound terms, outside a certain framework, within certain limits.

But the simple fan of tarot or rather, if I can call him - the reader -, there is no doubt, while he handles his cards, turns them over and shuffles them, he is convinced that he is witnessing the real development of things, of which he has only seen the surface up to now, as if he had placed a readable translucent paper onto the keys to the world, no matter what hidden events are suddenly revealed in his face, in his imaginations, in his particular reasoning, the tarot occupies that place, as in the times, of the Augur and Sibyl, from the three-foot pedestal, the sensitive young virgin, almost sleepwalking - sometimes the maid, this young girl – like in the times of Mesmer informs the whole family every night about the origin of evil, the passages through hell and the treatment of joint pain.

I. THE ARCANA AND THE LAW OF SPECIALTY

The Tarot constitutes a language, of which we are only given the alphabet. This alphabet comprises seventy-eight cards that appear as cryptograms or hieroglyphs. At first glance they present something evident and mysterious at the same time; something naive, but subtle. One sees in them a high priest, a crayfish, the sun and the moon, a juggler, a hanged man. It is an alphabet, where each letter - as we sometimes wish, totally in vain however – seem already to have their meaning. However, the outcome, the literary produce, of this language vanishes as soon as it is formed; through very different genres of play, some of whom are called; *Grand jeu*, *Petit jeu*, *Tirage Moyen*, *Grand Tirage*, *Accomlissement*, and all the rest.

On one hand, the tarot is nothing more than a common playing card game - just as French is a somewhat more evolved version of Latin, or Malay a primitive form of Malagasy. It is disputed, without great evidence, what purpose the early Tarot served. The fact is that both applications served the same purpose: either for the pure and simple gaming, for the prize or for the winnings - in some places it is the game of Lombard or the game of Tarrochino, and in others places Piquet or the Imperial game, or finally for the inquiry into one's destiny. From the game to the inquiry, every kind of mixture one can imagine. The player stuck in the café, shaking in front of his cards, throwing a sideways glance, and later, shouting out: "Only the scoundrels have any luck!" (the scoundrel being his adversaries), or: "Decidedly, the good Lord himself is against me!" He is concerned with winning a round of drinks. He questions the Gods and desires to shame them.

Since the use is the same, the cards are analogous; the same courts, kings, queens (or ladies), jacks (in the tarot, equipped with horses). The same numbered cards; ace, two, three, four, and so on up to ten. The "suits" are here simply; Clover, Diamonds, Hearts and Spades, and in tarot; Clubs, Coins, Cups and Swords. However, there is a more noticeable difference too. Those are the twenty-two Major Arcana - they are also called "Trumps" of the Tarot, which outrank, in gameplay, any other card and in card divination they indicate the greater intentions of destiny.

10

This is not an abnormal or surprising difference. Linguists usually distinguish between synthetic and analytical language. They surmise that it is common to see an analytic language return to synthesis or synthetics, towards analysis by reason of the law of specialty. This is why in French someone would say *plus pur*, where in Latin with a single word one would say *purior* or *á l´amour* as appose to in Latin just *amori,* and *de l'arbre* instead of *arboris. From, to* or *more* are called exponents. They are used on most of the old nouns, adjectives or adverbs, which have been extracted from the old common language and now endowed with an active force.

Likewise, as with the Major Arcana, in the current playing cards, each suit can become a Trump. It depends, on the game, on the player's luck during a round or the decision of the player - who at the price of a concession, gets a winning round in the game. However, in Tarot, the Trumps form a separate branch. They do not depend on any suit. They are provided with names and numbers. In other words, they are beyond exponents, each one seems to mark, going forward, as happen with the prepositions, its particular nuance and in the whole, a common intention.

II. DISORDER AND METAMORPHOSIS

What is the intention? If I look patiently at these unique pictograms, what amazes me above all, is their diversity. It would seem that everybody has been called in to collaborate here, as well as all mythologies. (How are they to be understood?) That Devil accompanied by two little devils, that final Judgment, with its blowing trumpet and the resurrection of the bodies, come directly from Christianity, but, the Popess? Here there is an air of blasphemy. On the other hand, some say, she is Isis on her knees, with the great book of nature (which she is not reading); behind her an extended vail. Also, the Wheel of Fortune, with its Sphinx, its monkey and its dog, refer to

11

Egypt. However, Cupid, Strength, the triumphal Chariot evokes in us the Greeks and the Romans. There are more precious references too, the crayfish (or cancer), the twins, Pleiades, obviously refer to astrology. The Pope between the Jachin and Boaz columns, to the Masonic initiation, the transmutation of metals, to medieval alchemy.

Other images seem to simply evoke proverbs; Temperance throws water into its wine; the Star (but why *the* star?) carries water to the river, dogs bark at the moon. In short, these are not religions or scientific matters, that are reached here. It is, as if, the unknown author of the tarot had come to some knowledge, that would recognize their profound unity, which encompasses them all in the same vision. Or, if you prefer, that he has taken advantage of, by the grace of God, for his collection of images, so the mess of beliefs and myths where all merged into one. One must analyse them more closely.

However, each card, in its own way, offers, in depth, the same disorder. Is that old man disguised in a red cape, a blue coat, and a yellow tiara really the Pope? (He should be white, as we all know). And why does Death cut heads and hands already buried (or would it be a second death?) and the Hanged man, where does his triumphant air come from, that party costume and looking at the card - is he hanging by one foot? - his dancing aspect perhaps? Why is the Devil a hermaphrodite? What about the Juggler? Being placed on a deserted mountain, is not the custom of Jugglers. Why is this air of inspiration, a symbol of infinity? Is this tarot card itself a juggler or a fortune teller? Is he God? The Fool is the only one in the Arcana that has no number, as if madness threatens the player - or the initiate – at any moment perhaps? The Name. Why do certain names deceive us? The eighteenth Arcanum, has as its subject the moon (as labelled) - or perhaps that mysterious crayfish that appears only vaguely, blue in blue water, but our eyes do not seem to detach from it. Likewise, in the seventeenth Arcanum, the star gives way to the young girl

12

with two jugs; the Sun in Arcanum nineteen, to twins. Why do the two boys falling from their tower, seemingly without reason, show such pleasure when hitting the ground? The fortune on its wheel of transformation as represented in the last Arcanum, as you look more closely, into that androgyny rising to the heavens (is that the soul finally liberated?) does it lead to the Juggler and his magic staff? It seems that the cycle never ends.

III. ON THE TREATMENT OF OCCULT FACTS

To those who take into account secrets or matters of the occult - apparitions, hauntings, premonitory dreams, lucky charms, telepathy, telekinesis, ghosts - two points will first of all become evident.

Here is the first: observed (or practiced) in all places and during all times by spiritual people - not necessarily from fantasy or chimerical spirits as claimed by some writers (and even sages), no, but for the most part from a solid and practical point of view and with your feet planted on the ground; by hunters and fishermen, peasants, soldiers. A complete falsehood would be an even more unbelievable (or if you prefer, occult) phenomena than their apparitions. I would even ask a more difficult question. Because it remains to be explained how so many people, otherwise honest and of good sense and of a rather distrustful nature, have been able, without having consulted in any way, to commit to an identical error in union with thousands and thousands of others. The sages pay great attention, in their method, to the principle of economics, which consists in classifying the questions as serious and not dismissing any issues out of hand, unnecessarily. Well, economics here consists simply in admitting once and for all, that there are phenomena that are beyond the measures of reason, as well as in the control of science; occult phenomena, in no way vain or gratuitous; but for those of us who participate (in the

13

absence of knowing them) in the events of the world; in the origin of evil, the landscapes of hell - perhaps even in the treatment of joint pain - from where the best and most irrefutable proof would be, if you like, this: One does not become, one is not, a savant by knowledge, nor reasonable through reason, but through a choice, which is rather of the order of mystery or of faith: By an occult choice made very articulately.

A second point to consider and not less obvious: There have been no shortages of men, who have had apparitions over the ages, hauntings and such. There have been those who have tried to dismiss the laws and rules and have been able to divert the beneficial effects to their advantage, as well towards evil ends. Now, the science and techniques that have resulted from their efforts have a curious trait in common: They all go wrong quite quickly. No matter how plausible their issue may be, no matter how accurate their first data. They are persecuted and often die in an extremely pretentious, unworthy way, summarily quite empty and in vain. Despite our painful, efforts of progress, we hardly know now more about apparitions and miracles than the Chinese did in the tenth century BC. We simply know "they exist".

The last that needs to be said of the occult specialists is that they come off badly, even faster than their sciences. I dare not even think of those who were shipwrecked in misery, or infected with disease; Court de Gebelin, Eliphas Levi or the gypsies, whose mysterious mission seem to have consisted in spreading the Tarot throughout the world, having barely benefited from the riches, that they graciously promise us.

And the darkest, the occultists we know best - those whom the century of enlightenment saw: Saint-Germain, Cagliostro, Mesmer, Casanova, and a little later Etteila -, generally end up living at the expense of naive old ladies, desirous of immortality. In short someday, they end up as famous mediums to people they deceive, unless they adopt the profession that seems to go better with that of a fortune teller; secret agents, spies; or also researchers, benefiting the state, that pays them with ditches, that laudable desire to find hidden treasure.

Thus, there are occult facts and the least that can be said is; that these facts are not allowed to be mastered, nor fully known; they do not do science. They dissolve or get lost, as soon as they are brought up to date. In short, they are not to be found, but doubly so, essentially occult. Such is precisely the common sense of the Arcana, and their insistence.

Was it necessary for so much consideration and care in mind, in the application of the meaning of the words used? Absolutely. Suffice to say, the Tarot evokes the mess that has run high among us, and the current purpose of which, more or less, is that the occult demands to be explained, revealed, communicated: Let it stand, without losing its virtue, the light of day. There is not much more foolish (or more disgusting) that aspires to serve our interests. Opposing this is what the lovers of Tarot maintain, that the secrets are in no way a chance nor an accident; it is not a simple flaw. Not, specifically a thing, rather as nature.

Where does the particular reading method originate in this book? It would be unwise to treat this book as a physics or geometry manual. Quite the opposite. You don't have to memorize it. Nor show it - even if it is in my opinion, very accurate and very beautiful - to all your friends. Certainly, you have to read it, but forget it immediately after, and later read it again (without ever rereading it). In a word, relegating it to that secret part of ourselves, where the entire Tarot is nothing but a constant allusion.

JEAN PAULHAN

15

EXPOSE

If an attempt were made to demonstrate to a man of science, the value and the divinatory properties of the Tarot, it is probable, that this demonstration would be met with scepticism, if not irony, since the Tarot would provoke in him the memory of card readers, or if you prefer; fortune tellers, and he would regard it entirely, as a product of superstition and a means of exploiting human credulity.

Perhaps he would change his mind considering that one should challenge one's preconceptions, that possibly a survivor from the past, such as the Tarot, tenacious as it is, hides an original and a deep meaning, which has been clouded by conceptions of the present. Perhaps, when remembering that the Tarot is the precursor for the playing cards, which are, one of the principle instruments for the passions of gaming, would he not look for the causes of the role they play in humanity, and would he not like to know, why man subjects himself to the randomness of their combinations, in the hope of achieving fortune, when all too often he gains nothing but disappointments? And would he not be prompted to wonder, whether this appeal from these man-made cards, does not stem from some profound source?

The answer will be given, if one takes the trouble to examine how man comes to knowledge. Then he will recall, that the logical systems he employs in the pursuit of knowledge are primarily reasoning by identification and reasoning by analogy. The first serves as a basis for modern science, from which mathematics and most of the branches taught in our scientific schools derive. The second is used by nature, she ignores the so-called exact sciences, which are really nothing but methods of abstractions, conceived by our minds, chosen by us, because their mechanisms easily adapts to the imperfections of our faculties. Nature does not accept rigorous reasoning, whose lack of flexibility would paralyze her efforts, because she never creates two identical things. She knows only qualities, and to coordinate these qualities with each other, she bases it on analogies and proceeds with affinity.

Thus, to know the laws and principles of nature, one would have to determine the analogical links that connect all things. But this operation, due to the complexity and immensity of the elements it encompasses, surpasses the scope of human understanding, so that it cannot be verified except by limiting it to the study of the simplest and most accessible link; to our spirit. Now, those who fulfil these conditions must enter the framework of tangible things, and consequently take on the aspect of forms with which we are familiar. That can then serve as a base and allow for a glimpse of the other levels by their similarities. This is why man has been forced to resort to symbolism, that is, to the transposition of cosmic laws onto the physical world, concretizing them in the form of pictorial scenes. Such are the causes that have led men of time past to conceive the images of the Tarot.

What knowledge do we have on the origins of the Tarot and about the vicissitudes, it has suffered through the ages in form and in interpretation?

A chronicle of Giovanni de Juzzo de Caveluzo, preserved in the archives of Viterbo, fixes the time when the cards first appeared in Europe, in the following passage: "In the year 1379 was introduced in Viterbo the game of cards which came from the land of the Saracens and which is called Naïb among them." This shows that the cards have a very foreign origin. If we put historical writings aside and look to the oral traditions and to certain books, as those by Paravey[1], or Moreau de Dammartin[2], the Tarot goes back to the Egyptians, who in turn may have gotten it from previous peoples. We may suppose that the elites of these peoples, in contemplation of the heavens, perceived in the groupings of stars and in the movement of planets, the discovery of cosmic laws, which with their sense of symbolism is expressed in a series of images. Each one of them, through the arrangement of their colours, objects, and figures, their implications highlighting the principles that their authors had recognized. Their number and sequence was determined by the rules of analogy, and the set, which has been given the name Tarot, constituted a synthesis, that summarized the evolution of the universe. According to the authors we have cited, these images, schematized to their maximum, would have been the origins of the hieroglyphic writings. Moreau de Dammartin, in support of these ideas, groups several constellations and depicts them in the sky in such

---

[1](Le Chevalier Charles-Hippolyte de Paravey, French Orientalist, 1787-1871. *Differents ouvrages*; Summary of the handwritten memoirs, manuscripts, concerning the origin of Earth, age of the Zodiac etc. *Paris 1835*. Confirmation of the Bible and the Egyptian and Greek traditions, through the hieroglyphic books discovered in China. *Paris 1838*. Astronomical knowledge of the ancient peoples of Egypt and Asia on the moons of Jupiter and the rings of Saturn. *Paris 1835*. Hieroglyphic documents seized in Assyria and preserved in China and America concerning the first flood of Noah. *Paris 1838*. Essays on the unique origin of the hieroglyphs, of numbers and letters of all people, preceded by a quick glance at the History of the World, between the age of Creation and the age of Nabonassar, and about certain ideas on the formation of the first writings, which existed before the Deluge, and which became the Hieroglyphic system. *Paris, Treuttel et Wurtz, Paris 1826*. Hieroglyphic Astronomical illustrations, of the planispheres and the Zodiac discovered in Egypt, in Caldea, in India and in Japan, *Delabaye Paris 1835*. A new Consideration on the Planispheres of Denderah, *Paris, Treuttel et Wurtz, 1835*. On the Spheres and the Constellations of Ancient Hieroglyphic Astronomy, etc. *Paris 1835*.)
[2]Hieroglyphical Characters of All Nations. Origin of the shape of the characters in the alphabet, Chinese characters, the Egyptian hieroglyphics etc. *by Moreau de Dammartin, member of the Historic Institute, Paris, 1839.*

18

a way, that they represent "The Juggler" and some other cards of the Tarot, while simultaneously applying the corresponding letters of the alphabet.

However, it may be, according to oral tradition, that the Tarot cards constitute a pictorial representation of the history of the world, and their combinations express the undulating and diverse play of universal forces. That is why the person who handles these cards believes with their shuffling, if done with affinity, with the mental or passionate projection of the querent, can reveal the cosmic law at play, and reveal, to a certain extent, his destiny.

The consequence of these origins has been to present the Tarot in three aspects; one symbolic, another divinatory, and the third to multiple card combinations. Three streams result from this; the initial, accessible only to the analogical mind, represents the Tarot proper; the second, called fortune-telling, used by the cartomancer, a translation from the figures, a degraded form from the original Tarot; the third, which does not concern itself with more than the choosing and the handling of combinations, constitutes the playing cards.

This triple current has given birth to innumerable images, that vary by the details of the objects, by the nature of the characters, by the philosophical, ritual or humorous qualities they have been attributed. Nevertheless, they all relate more or less faithfully or fancifully to the principles of the Tarot. This is how, setting traditional playing cards aside, there are either a multitude of decks containing representations of scenes; historical, political or with satirical figures, or groups of symbolic images suitable for the facilitation of divination, such as those of Mademoiselle Lenormand, whom it is said, had predicted Bonaparte his destiny; or, drawings intended to reconstruct the original Tarot, both according to personal inspiration and according to data from ancient works, such as those of Etteila, Eliphas Levi, Papus, Stanislas de

Guaita, and by Oswald Wirth, made in the last century and in the beginning of this one.

What is one to think of this mountain of images, which ones are the most interesting? Is there one among them that stands out and deserves special attention? It was up to Paul Marteau to settle this question.

Paul Marteau, a grand master *cartier* of France, is one of the directors of the House of Grimaud, whose fame, in the manufacture of card decks, is worldwide. He knows everything that has been said or done with these cards. It is enough to enter his office, walls plastered with decks of all kinds and of all times, to attest to his competence in such a matter. He knows their value and he knows how to bring out all their peculiarities with humour. But, in his eyes, no deck is comparable to the old Tarot called "de Marseille", because, according to him, it is the most consistent with tradition, the richest in analogical meanings, but due to its crude design and the obscurity of its symbols, which can only be rediscovered through careful analysis, have been made unknown. Paul Marteau found it useful to draw attention to it, and present its interpretation to the public.

That is why, first of all, he reissued it with such care, and then composing this book, in which he is interested in showing the reader, that nothing in this Tarot has been left to chance, that the images have been conceived in such a way that they give a sense to the smallest details, that the colours are always appropriate to the main idea of each Arcanum, and that the whole thing reveals a transcendental philosophy. Therefore, his work does not contain a history of the cards, not even a criticism of the conception of the Tarot de Marseille. He only translates its symbolism.

A delicate operation, which is easy to realize after having examined the difficulties of the problem. The available means that can be taken as a starting point or support are poor. As a starting point, there are some rules of symbology however: It is known, for example, that in general yellow signifies intelligence or the spiritual, blue the psyche or the mystical state, red the passions or appetites. Supporting this, there are commentaries published on similar Tarots, however in addition to the fact that for the most part they do not refer to more than the 22 Major Arcana and leave the 56 Minor Arcana in the shades, they hardly go beyond the philosophy of their authors and their images are incomplete or distorted, because they have neglected to represent, what they have misunderstood. In other words, little is known about the origins of the Tarot de Marseille. Certain characteristics of the images, the shape of the dress and the shape of the faces, suggest that it dates back to the mid-15th century and that it was made in Germany. According to occult tradition, it would be a reproduction, adapted to the dress of the time, of a more ancient Tarot belonging to the Greeks of Phocis - the ancient Marseille -, which they in turn acquired from the Egyptians.

In the presence of such little information, it is necessary at times to proceed with a meticulous analysis, and sometimes by synthesis, in order to interpret the smallest nuances of the images and organize them, so that the result forms a coherent and rational whole. This meticulous work is still insufficient, when one considers that the Tarot, in order to express all the flexibility of the laws of nature and the cosmos, it proposes to reflect. One has to adapt the elements of the images, colours, shapes and presentations, to the particular meaning of each card, and this without diverting from their original meaning. White, for example, a synthesis of all colours, indicates, among other nuances, the abstract, nothingness or repose. The abstract, if the card approaches it as a symbol of the universal. Nothingness or a negation, if it is placed in the material and tangible point of view, where the abstract does not exist. Rest, if the card is related to an idea of action or inertia. Red already signifies the merging of the soul into matter, already, in a more concrete sense, the impulsiveness of instinct and of animal passions. This results in a multitude of nuances, that are not only difficult to appreciate, but also surpass the means of expressing them in the French language, however rich it may be.

Another difficulty resides in the magnitude of meanings a given symbol has. Because, to interpret a symbol, is to find by analogy, the idea that is linked to this or that pose, or this or that contour. More precisely, it is to establish the passage from the concrete to the abstract, but this step goes from the most down to earth sense, to the one that rises to the highest of metaphysics, and travels from this extreme to the other by an indefinite series of levels. Let us consider, by way of example, the first four Arcana of the Tarot, that form a set; the Juggler (*Bateleur*), the Popess (*Papesse*), the Empress (*Impératrice*), the Emperor (*Empereur*) and let us interpret them predominantly in their higher sense.

The Juggler means the first emanation, and consequently represents the nebulous laws that govern their development. The Popess symbolizes the universal matrix, and from the book on her lap, which describes all the cosmic combinations, she extracts the ideograms, which she projects into space, and which become the germs of worlds. The Empress is the universal fate and weaves the threads of cosmic destinies, with which the Emperor builds worlds.

In its inferior and concrete meaning corresponding to human work, the Juggler means nothing more than a setting out on a path, the result of which will be indicated by the cards that surround him. The Popess becomes something unexpected that arises. The Empress is a gestation, an unknown factor, whose adjustments must be expected, and the Emperor is a domination over the unstable, an ephemeral power, a temporary regime.

Another interpretation of the cards can also be obtained, it is purely abstract, by interpreting through

22

analogy the meaning of the numbers inscribed on the top of each card. The 1 (the Juggler) means the beginning of all things, the primordial principle, the action taken in its essence. The 2 (the Popess) constitutes, on the contrary, the essence of passivity, because of the two units that compose it, from a qualifying point of view, when taken in reverse, are opposed to themselves. Through this shock, they create a movement in place, a dynamic stabilization, which symbolizes any substance of mystery she contains, and which is due to the effects of her receptivity to universal forces. The 3 (the Empress), which characterizes the notion of "succession" (1 + 1 + 1), symbolizes the evolutionary step from one plane to another, that is, in the Trinity, the current that goes from father to son and from son to father through the Holy Spirit. The 4 (the Emperor), or 2 versus 2, indicates a double polarity, which, depending on whether they oppose each other or whether they are reconciled, are represented by the square or the cross, expressing matter with its four elements (fire, air, water and earth) or the balance of forces in constructive action.

Between these extremes multiple transitions can be established. Paul Marteau couldn't even think of covering them all. He had to make a choice and stay in an arena accessible to the public and susceptible to interest. He stopped on the path of the psyche, just as the Tarot had drawn him to it; meaning, in the oscillations of the human soul between the bonds of matter and the call of the Divine.

To this limitation is added another; the Tarot subordinates its philosophy to that of numbers; that is to say, to its analogical laws. Logic would have wanted Paul Marteau, in order to make his deductions understood, be as previously made on the presentation on the symbolism of numbers. In doing so, it would have satisfied readers concerned with seeing the interpretations rest on narrow logic. Apart from the fact that this work would have been

23

tedious in its abstractions, it would have required an additional volume; thus, he had to reduce his exposition on the numbers to what was strictly indispensable for the understanding of the Tarot.

Besides, criticism is easy in a domain that does not include the rational form of our contemporary sciences. For this reason, I repeat, Paul Marteau has not wanted to undertake a reasoned study of the Tarot in general, nor to criticize what may be good or defective, complete or incomplete, in the Tarot de Marseille, he has sought out its significance and has exposed it to the reader, to allow him to appreciate for himself a work, that human wisdom has conceived through the centuries.

EUGÈNE CASLANT

(École Polytechnique)

INTRODUCTION

The tarot is a set of images, that symbolically expresses the work, man needs to undergo in his own evolution. In other words, to his purpose, what is inscribed in his destiny. An evolution that will require struggles, efforts, joys and sufferings according to whether or not, he agrees with the universal laws.

Having chosen the Tarot which best expresses this journey; the Tarot de Marseille[3], one will find the symbolic interpretation of it in this book.

*

The 78 cards of this Tarot are presented with two different classifications; the first 21 cards + 1, traditionally called the Major Arcana, and then the 56 Minor Arcana, which are broken down into four series of 10 cards, followed by four courts.

*

In order to make a symbolic interpretation of these cards, each Major Arcanum makes use of, except for the Fool, a number at the top, an image whether human, animal or an object in the centre and a name at the bottom, except for Arcanum XIII.

---

[3] This Tarot is the one that was edited in 1761 by Nicolas Conver, master card maker in Marseille, who had preserved the woodblocks and colours of his distant predecessors. This Tarot is currently being published by B.P. Grimaud, who took over from Conver and could thus continue the printing of the traditional Tarot, in its original form.

*

The 10 Minor Arcana of Swords, of Cups and of Clubs, with the exception of the Aces, display a number and no name. The 10 Arcana of Coins, neither number, nor name; while the 16 Courts that follow do not have numbers only generic names.

*

The number, taken symbolically, reveals the philosophical principles, that allow us to understand the language of the makeup of the Cosmos, with its laws and principles. The meanings each number can represent are infinite. The comparisons of the principles represented by the number with the figure itself, makes it possible to specify the point of view, from which it has been contemplated, equally so, the qualities of its colours, the relative arrangement of the objects and the particular meaning, which presides over the image on the card, provides a basis for interpretation.

*

The colours of the figures´ clothing that may seem inconsistent, the apparent naivety of Tarot figure design, are not, as some commentators seem to suppose, errors or work of negligence, but rather conceal a very precise symbolic value, that one should not cease to explore.

*

Finally, the name, due to its specific nature, symbolizes the concrete and tangible aspect, that the card can represent, when its principle meaning is given by the number. The study of this name will allow, therefore, to specify the tangible meaning of each card.

*

Thus, each Major Arcanum will be studied in the following order:

-   In an analogic sense, of the particular number, specifically as it relates to the card or principle;
-   The derived abstract[4] meaning, which gives the general quality of the card;
-   An interpretation of the symbolism of the main object on the card;
-   The description of the details, through the interpretation of its attributes, colours and the particulars on the card;
-   The Orientation of the figure;
-   The meaning of the name used on the card, its application in the concrete, this meaning however being subordinated to its abstract meaning.

Given that the number of positive significations are too great in number to be determined; it will be necessary to limit oneself, to give a few meanings to each of the elements of the human ternary, chiefly: The "Mental" or intelligence, the "Animistic"[5], that is, the emotional, passions, and finally the "Physical", the utilitarian aspects of life. Then, as everything has its opposite, the meaning will be suggested, when the card is inverted. This will then

---

[4] The general meaning of the principle, which we shall call *abstract*, as opposed to its tangible or utilitarian meaning, which we shall call *concrete*.

[5] Translator: Please note, Marteau uses the word *animistic* (*animique*) throughout this book. Marteau reads into this word several meanings; feelings, passions, appetites, animation, life energy and more, and despite the word, generally not in a spiritual way. It has not always been clear, when he means what. I have therefore intentionally avoided giving a specific translation to this word.

conclude by assigning a definition of the elementary meaning of the card.

*

As the circumstances in where the Major Arcana have been studied are modified by the introduction of the Minor Arcana, a new study, the symbolism of numbers, on one hand, and of the suits, on the other, must be examined before any further interpretation.

*

The Tarot is a universal vibrating instrument and becomes a source of energy through the fluidic projections of our thoughts. By giving us the symbolic keys of the universal laws, that preside over the destiny of man, the Tarot allows us to make associations from these currents and, consequently, foresee certain events by analogy or affinity. In order to allow a party to the cards to see along these lines, of the method of use, it is finally presented here, to make possible the deductions from Tarot combinations, the implications relating to all momentary concerns, as established by the card spread, as well as the elementary rules that allow one to make useful deductions.[6]

PAUL MARTEAU
Paris, 1928 – 1948

---

[6] The reader will kindly excuse the repetitions and the somewhat heavy phraseology. It is difficult to translate the abstract into the concrete, while remaining faithful to the interpretation of the substantive idea. The various words that can be used are few in number and overused. You might want to regard this book, as a kind of dictionary or even an encyclopaedia, where you will find the explanatory details of each card.

ORIENTATION OF FIGURES AND SYMBOLISM OF BODY PARTS[7]

The orientation of the figures indicates the nature of the action[8]. Depending on whether the figure is seen from the left profile, from the front or from the right profile, there is meditation, reflective action, direct action or evolution, meaning a restrain of action. If the figure is standing, there is an indication of latent work and it is in an active mode; activity, command, energy. If it is sitting, its action is exercised passively; inertia, resistance or internal elaboration. In this interpretation, the head plays the leading role, because it symbolizes the inclination or the will. If, for example, the body is facing forward and standing, the head turned to the left, as in the Juggler, there is a reflection taking place, before proceeding to the action, which has already been prepared to be direct.

The HEAD in the Tarot expresses the will, of command. The COVERED HEAD equates to figures who do not express their will in the physical. The headdress represents the issue, the will is manifested along the lines symbolized by it. For example, a crown represents a larger radiance, taking its origin from more subtle planes, owing to the rosettes on it, they constitute centres of attraction. The will here is more impersonal, than in the other headdresses, where instead, things generated by individual will are represented.

---

[7] The given descriptions are general, but they can be attenuated or accentuated by certain details on the figure's clothing.

[8] See footnote from the Juggler.

The HAIR expresses fluid emissions. If it is colourless, there is no great willpower, but if it is coloured, there is a greater manifestation of mental activity. If in colour gold, it represents a more formal, more concrete, a more accomplished mental realization. If in colour blue, the force is enclosed in the spiritual and tends to decrease.

HAIR IN DISORDER is an indication of a will with great power behind it.

HAIR CAREFULLY STYLED has no particular meaning; the demonstration of will is more contained; for example, by "The Justice", who is mentally fairly accomplished.

A BEARD indicates the will, a wilful and a more focused concentration.

The NECK is a link between the mental (head) and the animistic (chest); UNCOVERED, indicates a simple communication between both planes; COVERED, reinforces, according to its colour, the difference between animistic intensity and mental intensity.

The NECK should be supported at its base in order to avoid bad composure and bad dispositions. Completely uncovered, represents freedom and independence.

The TORSO represents the animistic aspect, buttons and ornaments are animistic enrichments, peculiarities: If the dress is of two colours, the animistic has a double meaning. The entire torso represents animism, with its spiritual aspect on the chest, and its material aspect on the belly, such as maternal love vs. instincts.

The BELT is the animistic aspect that deals with reasons of will; man does not just give up, but finds reasons for his impulses and actions.

The ARMS indicate intelligent, reasoned actions; they are interpreters of the mental and the animistic (the colour indicates whether the mental outweighs the animistic).

The LEFT ARM the left arm is the transmission of the altruistic and the affective animistic messages, the psyche that directs it.

30

The RIGHT ARM transmits the decisions, the will, the hopes, the leading to action.

The LOWERED ARM means an action that has produced its fruits or an impediment to act; "The Juggler's" lowered arm underscores his indecision and his modesty.

The RAISED ARM indicates the connection with the above, the capture of forces.

ARMS ON THE BELT represents the circulation between the animistic and the physical, as if to detach or let go, or to decide on something.

The LEGS indicate the realizations through action. If man is halted, the action is halted; crossed legs represents the waiting, the status quo.

If a FOOT is in the air, as with "The Emperor", it is the indication of a departure and of decision making.

THE MAJOR ARCANA

THE JUGGLER
(Le Bateleur)

PRINCIPLE

The number 1, an expression of universal positivity, symbolizes the primordial creative principle, within its multiple reali-zations. The manifestation of this power, situated at the origin of all things, makes it engender, through its repetition, all the universal active and passive forces, of which the other numbers are a representation of. This is the one, that particularizes and defines objects and phenomena in the world of senses.

GENERAL AND ABSTRACT MEANING

In the study which follows, the first card of the Tarot a reminder of the positivity of the primary, should make us imagine an active and creative power. This is why it is depicted as someone standing surrounded by certain tools allowing him to perform his activities. The symbolism of this first card expresses, therefore MAN AS AN ACTIVE AND CREATIVE POWER.

The qualities of this power are indicated by the appearance of this card, as much as in the details of the figure, his clothing and in the depicted objects.

At the dawn of his creation, man was projected onto Earth, surrounded by a world, naturally hostile, was reduced to an activity of conservation and defense. This spawned in him responses, that he strove to perfect. This ability he acquired over time, and is still in the process of developing. This has led us to compare, in the Tarot, man to that of the Juggler, forced, by his situation, continually to direct his attention on the phenomena of the world of the senses. These inclinations, manifested, give the first card its name; The Juggler.

It may be observed, first of all, that the Juggler is standing firm, with his feet planted on the ground, he has the magnetic influence of someone remaining modest. The wand, a symbol, like the scepter, of intellectual authority, he holds in his left hand, pointing to the sky, allowing him to maintain contact with the currents above, the organizers of terrestrial influences, while his right hand manipulates, with skill and discernment, the objects on the table. These are:

—The knife, bringing the Sword to mind, a symbol of effort, of difficulty, of struggle.

—The money, representing the Coins, symbol of acquisition and work to be carried out.

—The chalice, standing in for the Cup, a symbol of love, of good or bad passions and of sacrifice.

—Finally, the wand which he holds in his hand, an image of the Club, completing the four devices of the Tarot.

FEATURES BY ANALOGY

In general, one will take notice of the hat, in particular, which exterior is light green, indicating adaptation and mental[9] strength. The yellow or gold cap; wisdom. The red brim; material passions. The shape of it as a ∞, a symbol of infinity, of universal life, reminds us, that man is subject to the chains of universal harmonies of which he is also part.

The hair of the Juggler, white in its length and golden at its curly ends, designates wisdom as the fruit of age and experience.

His tunic above the belt is, on the left side blue and on the right red, and these colours are reversed below: The blue represents the psyche and the receptive aspects of his personality, and the red, the passionate and active aspects of his personality, each in balance with the other.

His belt is yellow, a mental link uniting wisdom and spirituality, and his collar white, for this spirituality must be subjected to intelligence, represented by the head.

His left arm is red on top, yellow in the middle and blue below. He is holding between his fingers a yellow wand; the arm is a symbol of gesture and power, and the left arm is directed by the psyche, since the material world, inert in of itself, only moves under the influence from gestures of the psyche.

His right arm is opposite to his left in colour, and he is holding between his fingers a yellow ball which

---

[9] Translator: Marteau uses the words *mental and psyche (psychique)* throughout this book. It is clear that he applies many different meanings to these words; mind, awareness, consciousness, psychological, psychic and more. It has not always been clear, when he means what. I have therefore intentionally tried, in some places, not to give a specific translation to these words. Also note Marteau, in general, attributes a higher spiritual quality to the word *mental* than *psyche*.

35

synthesizes the principles of cosmic matter. This arm is positioned lower to indicate, that man must subordinate his actions, as suggested by his right side, to the laws of the cosmos in the moment, he is in contact with them.

His legs, the left one blue with a red shoe and the right one red with a blue shoe, indicate that the right side must master the elements by balancing his psyche with his actions.

He holds a sphere in his right hand and, as depicted, appears to be a disk as much as it appears to be a ball. The Juggler is engendering this illusion and can present it, as he pleases, as flat or spherical. The ball represents a state of continuity; when presenting it as a disk, the Juggler is limiting its state, in this state it represents human Intelligence. As a ball, however, it is an expression of divine intelligence. The Juggler can, using his powers, present it, one way or the other. In other words, he can confine intelligence to the physical plane and keep it there, but he cannot do so on the plane of the psyche. It is for this reason that he shows the sphere in both aspects.

The table, in the colour of flesh, symbolizes the living, the material support, the Juggler can use in his schemes.

The bag with objects is yellow: scattered as they are, they have their own destiny, but will reunite in the bag, give up their individuality and re-establish unity by forming a complete composite, overseen by the mental.

The yellow cup represents mental power. It can contain the three yellow pieces, Trinity expressed as a mental element, and the four red pieces, divided into two sets of two, symbolize the double polarity. These constitute the four elements, the principle of the material world.

The isolated use of the red pieces reflects greed, the individual´s search for wealth, whereas the isolated use of the yellow pieces denotes the struggles of the higher mind. The simultaneous use of the three yellow pieces with the four red pieces creates a septenary, which exerts the radiance and power of divine intelligence allied with temporal intelligence.

The dice, a representation of chance, are yellow to show that divine intelligence always intervenes and that nothing happens by chance. The points marked on them point out what man calls chance is actually the combination of numbers, obeying laws so profound as to be invisible.

The knife represents the object which can cut the thread of life, but the blue colour of the grip indicates that it can only be used in an animistic way. For man is able to be a master or a slave of his destiny, depending on the state of his soul. Its sheath, also blue, signifies his freedom in the application of the knife. If man puts the knife back in its sheath, he renounces the power to eliminate flawed feelings and becomes a slave to himself.

The red cup is temporary power, of combinations; the dice are separated as with the knife, separated from their sheath.

The ground, yellow, represents the energies that need to be captured; the Juggler must rely on intelligence, and from this fertility will emerge, as symbolized by the green sprout.

These diverse elements are all invested in him, there is potential for evolution of matter through the spirit, but instead, they oblige him to struggle adverse hidden forces. If he trusts his wisdom, these forces will allow him to maintain his balance and in this way he can be the master of them, rather than be their toy.

ORIENTATION OF THE FIGURE

The pose of the Juggler standing, his body facing forward, his head turned to the left[10], indicates that reflection must precede direct action. He compares, makes a choice before acting.

PARTICULAR AND CONCRETE MEANING

The name of the card, THE JUGGLER, indicates the possibility of juggling many objects, meaning, managing one's circumstances with skill and making appropriate choices.

UTILITARIAN MEANINGS IN THE THREE PLANES

MENTAL. Ease in the combining of things, intelligent use of the elements, of subjects representing the mind.

ANIMISTIC. Matters of the psyche, that is, a tendency towards the search of sensation, represented by the vigor of the figure and by the quality of him as a creator. Generosity coupled with courtesy. Fertility in every way.

PHYSICAL. The green of the hat indicates, the physical plane, concerns of health; strong vitality and power over mental or nervous illnesses; obsessions or Neurasthenia. This card indicates a favorable trend, however since not explicit does not indicate healing. In order to interpret it, it

---

[10] When considering the pose of each figure, the situation is determined by how the card relates to the reader; for example, the head of the Juggler is regarded as turned to the left, while, in the world of illustrations, he would be looking to his right.

will be necessary to consider the other cards in the spread. Tendency of dispersion in action, due to the lack of unity in its quality, indicated by the infinite diversity of combinations, that can be made with all the objects that appear on the table. Hesitation. Indecision. Uncertainty in events.

INVERTED. Discussions, arguments which may turn violent, considering the power of the figure; flawed action, misguided undertakings.

*

In sum, in its elementary sense THE JUGGLER represents man in the presence of nature, with the power to master its currents.

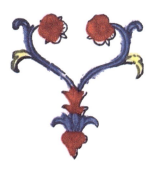

THE POPESS
(La Papesse)

PRINCIPLE

The number 2 is equal to 1 + 1. Unity being at the origin of the numbers, it can generate by successive additions, an increase in a series, therefore positive. Or facilitate a descending series, consequently negative. If both units are represented in the same direction, there is a collision and an arrest in the movement. If they are in opposing directions, there is polarity, the origin of movement and the foundation of something fruitful. The number 2, which synthesizes these two points of view, one of stop and the other of movement, symbolizes the fertility of nature, which is generally defined as stops and of plasticity.

GENERAL AND ABSTRACT MEANING

The figure on Arcanum II presents a massive figure in the shape of a veiled woman, wearing a tiara and thus corresponding to the universal fertile nature, sanctified; meaning, carrying in her a latent state, the cosmic power of reproduction. She can be considered as THE DIVINE

40

WIFE THROUGH HER ABILITY TO ENGENDER ETERNALLY AND FOR CREATION, THE ILLUSORY REALITIES OF THE MAYA.

Due to her passivity in the spiritual, she represents the mysteries, things hidden, she contains riches, which she keeps in her subconscious, as they are not externalized. The open book on her knees indicates, that it must be deciphered, perceived, rather than read, because her figure shows, her finger on a book, without looking, like a blind man feeling his way; it is the representation of the infinite possibilities of nature.

This card represents, therefore, things hidden, intuition, the understanding of the powers of nature. It is passive before the Juggler, but he has no power without her, because the active principle would be lost in infinity, if the passive principle that retains it, is not found. She wraps him in her protective mantle and gives shape to what he wants to create.

FEATURES BY ANALOGY

The significance of the colors on the costume can be related back to Arcanum I. The red robe[11] indicates the dominance of passions; the blue mantle, spirituality realized, subverting these passions, as well as covering and protecting her with religion and mysticism. The collar of the mantle its closure, and the yellow cords, are the ties that retain wisdom; bringing in spirituality and subjugating the passions for intelligence.

La Popess wears a gold tiara to show, that she is illuminated by solar radiance; meaning, by superior

---

[11] Translator: Please note the card shown from the Emrik & Binger deck, does not reflect Marteau´s text. The red and blue on the robe and mantle have been reversed.

wisdom, its three levels, loaded with precious stones, evoke the three worlds; physical, animistic and mental.

The physical circle, the lowest of the three, has rubies and topaz stones alternating. The rubies in the shape of four-leaf clovers, represent material activities. The topaz, a symbol of knowledge of universal laws, alternate with the rubies, but smaller in size, indicating Earth is only dimly illuminated by wisdom.

The animistic circle, which is placed in the middle, bears emeralds, which indicates knowledge in the domain of the psyche, and the two pearls that are in support, the sublimation of feelings, the suffering of the psyche, which leads to spiritual bliss.

The third circle, which has only a round crystal stone, cut like a diamond, symbolizes the pure mental and indicates through its round shape its role as the infinite; meaning, it has neither beginning nor end.

Under the tiara is a white headdress falling over her shoulders. The Popess is and should be a symbol of purity.

The flesh-colored veil behind the tiara shows that the upper part of this woman, a symbol of passivity, in a veil of matter may be hidden. It hovers around the tiara to make clear all the instability and mobility in the feminine principle, in face of rigidity in the wisdom indicated by the tiara, its qualities being immutable and eternal.

The opposition between the white headdress and the shaded veil explains how the feminine principle attracts sexual instinct from its need for motherhood, in as much so, its unconscious intentions remain pure.

The mantle can also be interpreted as an aspect of wisdom, but since it is unstable and capable of being worn and unworn, it cannot represent anything more than terrestrial wisdom.

The open book is flesh-colored to indicate, that it represents the evolution of life on the physical plane, not

42

only in all its forms, but also as a symbol of inheritance and of the continuance of the species.

The tiara and the book have very different interpretations: The open book shows the woman, taken to be a representative of the feminine principle, carrying within herself the knowledge of nature, but also that she can be its victim, in the moment, she allows herself to be covered by the veil of flesh, a symbol of the passions that imprison her and make her its slave. However she can equally represent the purity of nature, if she is able to preserve the purity of the white headdress. In that moment, she will be able to read the book, that reveals the knowledge of the past, of the laws of nature, on how to manage these laws, all the while, the tiara brings her the knowledge from the Above, indicated by the shine of precious stones.

Her feet are invisible because she must remain immobile, owing to her passivity.

ORIENTATION OF THE FIGURE

The position of the Popess, sitting, three-quarter to the left, indicates work, activity in concentration, calm and meditation.

PARTICULAR AND CONCRETE MEANING

The name of the card THE POPESS means; the highest principle of nature, of matter sanctified.

UTILITARIAN MEANINGS IN THE THREE PLANES

MENTAL. This card is very fruitful in the contribution of ideas. It solves problems, but does not suggest them.

ANIMISTIC. She is cold but friendly, welcoming, not affectionate.

PHYSICAL. Situation assured, power over events, revelation of things hidden, certainty in triumph over evil. Good health, weightiness.

INVERTED. Things slow down, she becomes more passive, nothing can be extracted from her anymore, she is a burden. Insights bring upset, intuitive revelations become false. Delay, stopping, difficulty in realizations.

*

In sum, in its elementary sense, THE POPESS represents nature, with its mysterious riches, which man must unveil and interpret.

THE EMPRESS
(L'Impératrice)

PRINCIPLE

The number 3 is equal to 2 + 1; meaning, the unity or the potential for action before a fertile undertaking, which consequently engenders fertility. Indeed, the card represents a seated woman, holding in her right hand the eagle, a symbol of creative imagination, and in her left hand a scepter, a symbol of creative power, crowned by a terrestrial globe, a representation of her power over matter.

GENERAL AND ABSTRACT MEANING

This card defines a harmonious set of + and -, by an activity in the passivity of matter, over which it has dominion and, conse-quently, a whole organized for the purposes of production and evolution,

45

that is, THE EVOLUTIONARY POWER OF FERTILE NATURE.

FEATURES BY ANALOGY

The golden globe of the scepter which the Empress holds in her left hand, resting on her arm, represents the universe, and the cross that crowns it indicates, that spirituality must dominate matter by penetrating it.

The shield that she holds firmly on the right depicts a yellow eagle on a flesh colored background. It indicates the intelligence acquired by itself by experiencing matter. Moreover, its position against her bust indicates, that she is inclined to master its great intuitions; however as the eagle, being no more than an image on a shield, more an expression of the imaginary than of reality. The shield, essentially mobile, indicates that it can be used for protection or be abandoned at will.

The Empress is seated, because she represents the power of the physical world, which is a state of immobility, and her invisible feet, as in the previous card, a confirmation of this. Her massive throne shows, by its color of flesh, that it is not there just for momentary support, but for definitive stability. It represents the roots of physical life.

Her crown comprising three gold spheres on a cap in red, requires of her mental powers. She is open to allow the mental by intuition to penetrate the material world, indicated by the red of the cap.

Her gold necklace is comprised of triangles, each one symbolizing; intelligence, matter and spirituality; through intelligence and by matter, they manifest spiritually in all domains, the whole must unite into one. The necklace represents the close coordination of these three states, which to reach perfection must not and cannot be separated.

46

The gold belt is the demarcation line in the parts of matter, between that of the inferior, non-intelligent and that of the superior, dominated by intelligence. The gold medallion with a triangle, connected to her necklace indicates, that when matter is dominated by intelligence, spirituality is emitted, forming a whole.

We do find, as in the preceding card, with the red of robe[12] the dominance of passions, but only up to her knees, the rest being in blue i.e. spirituality.

The tufts of yellow grass is an indication of passive fertility.

ORIENTATION OF THE FIGURE

The position of the Empress, sitting, from the front, indicates a clean cut and continuous activity in passivity.

PARTICULAR AND CONCRETE MEANING

The name of the card THE EMPRESS means the passive powers of the material world.

UTILITARIAN MEANINGS IN THE THREE PLANES

MENTAL. Penetration into matter through knowledge of practical things.

ANIMISTIC. Penetration into the soul of man. Fertile thoughts, creativity.

---

[12] Translator: The card shown may not reflect Marteau´s text. Although the robe is blue, the Empress´ sleeves are red.

PHYSICAL. Hope, balance. Solutions provided for problems, Improvement and renewal of a situation, compelling and continuous power of action.

INVERTED. Conflicts, arguments on all levels, everything gets mixed up and is confusing. Delay in some accomplishment, yet inevitable.

*

In sum, in its elementary sense, THE EMPRESS represents the fertile power of matter, made available to man for his creations.

THE EMPEROR
(L'Empereur)

PRINCIPLE

The number $4 = 2 + 2 = 2 \times 2 = 2^2$, this is, the fundamental operations of Arithmetics. It is the only number which possesses this property, which makes it synthetic and gives it an integral multiplicity in combinations. Therefore 2 is found twice in the 4 with three different characteristics; in essence, 2 presents matter as halting and as being plastic, one aspect of the 2s accentuates this notion of stopping, consequently, that of matter itself, just as the other aspect of the number 2 represents the active side of matter, in all its aspects and with all its combinations.

One can, in other words, regard this double 2 as forming a cross shaped polarity, one passive, the other active, which in combination guarantees a balance. 4 signifies therefore a balanced power in matter.

GENERAL AND ABSTRACT MEANING

Card IV shows a man, therefore an active principle, but remaining passive since he is in a sitting position, and as he is clearly in profile, facing left, he is giving himself over to reflection, to meditation, and to discernment.

It represents THE ACTIVE POWER OF MATTER and, consequently, its changes and transformations, because this activity never leaves something immobile. This is the result of a mental influence subordinated to the principles of the cosmos. It operates through the impressions it makes on consciousness, more than through direct action; it generates life on the spiritual and biological planes.

The Juggler and the Popess represent the two poles of the spiritual world, the Empress and Emperor the two poles of the material world.

The Empress symbolizes the passive domain of matter, the Emperor the active domain. The Empress emphasizes evolution, the Emperor manifests its structure. This card therefore denotes a state which has been achieved, a realization.

FEATURES BY ANALOGY

The meaning of the sceptre is the same as in the preceding card on the Empress; the sphere of gold crowned by a cross shows the power of matter, when it is penetrated by spiritual influence. This is a sign of scientific knowledge. Without this quality, the sceptre would be without any power, because all science which is not animated by spirituality is sterile. The Emperor holds the sceptre in his right hand because it is the positive pole; the Empress holds hers in her left to it is the negative pole; the set of the two cards together create a balance between these poles. The Emperor holds his sceptre before him to affirm his actions, while the Empress lets hers rest against her shoulder to emphasize her passivity. The Emperor's sceptre also indicates that his thinking is by justice and harmony, without any equivocation.

The positive pole represented by the Emperor can only animate matter when it is connected to the negative pole, as represented by the Empress. This is why the shield, a symbol of powerful intelligent outbursts acquired by man, rests on the ground at his feet, at his disposal, he makes no use of it, while the Empress holds hers against her abdomen, available, to ensure the birth of material creations.

The eagle depicted on the two shields is close to identical, the only difference being, the Empress's eagle has its head turned to the right and the Emperor's eagle is turned to the left, each one, on either side of the sceptre to indicate, that the idea that presides over the intellectual impulses is intuitive and inspired by the Empress, but are reasoned and desired by the Emperor. This is emphasized by the position of the wings on the eagle, raised upwards on the Empress' shield, while natural and symmetrical on the Emperor's shield, and wherefore, in the latter, the eagle brings an applied intelligence to practical things, its separated legs leave a gap, indicating it unites two separate entities; it establishes an equilibrium.

While the Empress is seated firmly on a throne, the Emperor is simply leaning back on a small flesh-coloured chair, in an unstable position to indicate that although he remains immobile, he is poised to stand up and is not as immovable as the Empress. He has only one foot on the ground: a symbol of his inclination to move, therefore to evolve, with the indication that the positive pole can only have intermittent contact with the material. He is wearing white shoes, a symbol of nothingness, thus underlining the fact that he cannot walk; the Emperor who seems to always be on the move, can neither move forward nor backward; it shows "immobility in action," an apparent contradiction which means that, although positive, therefore active, he is in matter that is fundamentally negative and holds him in his place, as indicated in the preceding paragraph.

His white collar, next to his head, is an indication that he is able to achieve an understanding by himself and that this supports his sterility if he remains insulated. This white collar also underlines the separation between the head and the body, specifying that in matter, the fall comes by means of the head, the animator´s principle.

His crown, similar to that of the Empress, has the same meaning.

His necklace consists of a golden cord; this braided tie is an adhesive and not that of bondage, like the one on the Empress. It shows that the positive pole, not being a spiritual state, can have nothing but a fragile bond with the spiritual. The joining ring on this necklace represents the principle of the circle, to which the Emperor must subordinate himself in order to bring about achievements.

His clothes, a tunic and breeches, are blue[13] finishing in white, on the collar and feet, denoting therefore a latent spiritual state, as the blue of his legs shows, that he is always able to go towards it and to achieve it. His red mantle indicates that he is enveloped in matter of which he is the animator.

His left hand is grabbing his yellow belt to show that he is able, through his psyche, to seize, to grasp the bond that attaches intelligence to the material plane, and to use it in order to exercise his domination over the material world.

The tuft of yellow grass has the same significance as in the preceding card, passive fertility, the yellow ground; the lever of wisdom.

---

[13] Translator: The card shown does not reflect Marteau´s text. The colours of the tunic are reversed; the mantle is blue and the tunic is red.

52

ORIENTATION OF THE FIGURE

The position of the Emperor, leaning against a throne, indicates passivity, the waiting prior to action, which with his raised foot indicates is imminent. It is a forthcoming realization, and every realization implies a result, a change. The Emperor makes decisions before acting.

PARTICULAR AND CONCRETE MEANING

The name of the card, THE EMPEROR indicates someone who judges action and who has the power to map out practical applications and to give useful council.

UTILITARIAN MEANINGS IN THE THREE PLANES

MENTAL. Balanced intelligence not exceeding what is useful for a plan of action.

ANIMISTIC. Agreement, peace, understanding, an agreement in opinions.

PHYSICAL. Transient goods, transient powers. Signature on a contract, the fusing of two or more groups, a given situation. A healthy balance but a tendency to be bloated.

INVERTED. Results contrary to those described above, everything fumbles, a disruption of balance. A fall, the loss of property, of health, or of control.

*

In sum, in its elementary sense, THE EMPEROR represents the material energies necessary for man to bestow onto his fleeting creations, in a moment of solidity.

THE POPE
(Le Pape)

PRINCIPLE

The number 5 = 4 + 1 indicating thus the unit of superior action or consciousness standing before matter, represented by 4; it has the power to act and to divert matter. The number 5 can also be defined as 2 + 1 + 2, the principle of unitary mediation between the two aspects of the material world; that which is inclined to stillness, and that which is inclined to action; between that which is inclined to the negative and that which rises above it, towards the positive. Card V, depicting the Pope before two figures, represents more specifically the second intention given to the number 5, that of the mediator.

GENERAL AND ABSTRACT MEANING

This Arcanum represents: THE PRINCIPLES OF SPIRITUAL POWER TRANSMITTANCE.

FEATURES BY ANALOGY

This card is a continuation of the Emperor since he dominates it, because the Pope represents the spiritual immensity which dominates the world, the spirituality in all things, and without it there can be no evolution. Without the Pope, the Emperor and the Empress would be negatives and remain sterile.

The Pope wears a crown identical to that of the Popess. His red robe, longer than that of the Emperor, shows that his power of action is more powerful and that he can cloak himself with matter at will, realizing thus, an act of concrete manifestation, permitting him to express himself in the physical. Its edges are gold and indicate, that he can restrict the tangible, meaning, intelligence surrounds it. It is equally the symbol of the presence of the divine spark in the concrete.

Under his red robe, he wears a blue tunic, indicating a potential for activities of the psyche.

The gold medallion pinned to his collar, in its centre a white crystal[14], shows his purity of intention.

His arms, dressed in white, imply abstinence from action and show that this card represents a mental symbol, that cannot act on the physical plane but through the mind.

He holds a cross of gold, with three crossbeams, representing the three worlds; the physical, the spiritual, and the mental, and equally symbolizing the temporal domain and the spirit of sacrifice. His left hand, wearing a yellow glove, marked by the seal of sacrifice, holding a cross, shows that he may not manage the cross without first appealing to his intelligence.

---

[14] Translator: Please note that the Pope, unlike on the card shown, in the Grimaud deck does not show this medallion in white, only in yellow or gold.

The two blue pillars situated behind the Pope represent, through the pillar on the right, the rise of action, and through the pillar on the left, the use of feelings. When these two poles are balanced through spirituality, they are based in an unshakable, solid foundation.

The two figures at his feet, symbolize the dualism of the forces which are in man, and which are able to turn towards good or evil, depending on whether they detach from matter or immerse into it.

The figure to the right of the Pope has a yellow tonsure, signifying intelligence, and flesh-coloured hair, indicating the physical plane. With his right hand turned down, he represents the descent into physical manifestation from where he administers the powers of good through spirituality, which he then directs by white magic, or the kind of magic permitted when overseen by higher intelligence (the yellow robe of the figure), or by spirituality (the blue hat). The red hood shows that he is able to cover himself for protection on the plane of passions.

The figure situated to the left of the Pope, whose hair and tonsure are flesh-coloured, represents the work on the plane of passions, towards his elevation into the spiritual plane, as indicated by his raised left hand.

The yellow stole sandwiched in his red robe signifies that the lowest life must, in order to elevate itself, always have a particle of intelligence embedded in it. This is the divine spark which permits it to evolve. The absence of a hat, shows that the spiritual cannot evolve in the material world directly, it can only act through an intermediary; the mind.

ORIENTATION OF THE FIGURE

The position of the Pope, facing the reader, sitting, underlines direct action through instruction. The two figures, seen from behind, facing in the opposite direction, have stopped in order to submit and give attention.

PARTICULAR AND CONCRETE MEANING

The name of the card indicates that THE POPE represents the one who receives divine inspiration and judges and instructs with absolute fairness.

UTILITARIAN MEANINGS IN THE THREE PLANES

MENTAL. The Pope, representing an active form of human intelligence offers purely logical solutions.

ANIMISTIC. Powerful feelings, deep affection, petitions which do not give way to sentimentality; it indicates normal feelings in circumstances where they occur.

PHYSICAL. Balance, security in a situation and in health. A secret revealed. Religious or scientific vocation.

INVERTED. The card of the Pope inverted is very unfortunate, as it indicates men left to their own devices and to their instincts, lost in confusion, because they have no spiritual support. A project delayed, a vocation coming late in life.

*

In sum, in its elementary sense, THE POPE represents the obligation, man has to apply divine teachings to his actions and submit to their laws.

THE LOVER
(L'Amoureux)

PRINCIPLE

The number 6 can be written like this (1 +2) + (1 + 2) in order to conform to the arrangement of the figures on this card. The number 2 by nature represents fertile passivity and the feminine principle. The two women thus constitute 2 + 2, while the masculine figure and cupid constitute two separate units, one in the plane below and one in the plane above. (1 + 2) + (1 + 2) represents the double current, both inclusive and evolving, detaching from matter or leading to it.

The grouping of elements on this card create a fusion between the spiritual and the material, because the two women converge onto the figure in the middle with an emanation of their material desires, with cupid representing the spark.

GENERAL AND ABSTRACT MEANING

The meaning of this card is THE FEELING OF PHYSICAL LOVE AND THE ENGENDERING OF SPIRITUAL LOVE, and it announces that love is the axis of evolution for man and for the creation of things. When love arises, the soul is exalted, and the spirit projects a spark toward the high, which immediately gives a response on a higher plane. This is symbolized by cupid, a representation of love drawing its bow on the top of the card.

The shock produced by this spark will bear its fruits and leave a foot print represented by the arrow, meaning, love, by elevating man above himself, allowing him in the physical plane some manifestations drawn from his own genius; liken to the musician, who finds in him his inspiration. Love is never sterile.

FEATURES BY ANALOGY

Interpreting symbolically the details of this card the emphasis is on the light rays, which emanate from cupid alternating in red, yellow, and blue, since the radiance of love acts out on all planes. The figure is flesh coloured to show his action with vital fluids. Cupid´s shoulder sash is both a tie and a mask; the tie between our dispositions toward flirting with earthly love, as well as to mask it with earthly sensations, always of divine essence, unable to take root in matter. It is fitted obliquely, and not by necessity. This shows that he cannot take prisoners, whatever the extent.

His blue wings show that the first idea of love is a burst towards mysticism, and his yellow hair, that the intelligence of love elevates man above matter.

The bow and arrow indicate speed and rhythm, for the arrow is a dynamic principle;

they are white, therefore negative, since the action love prefers is profoundly internal, more virtual than real.

The woman situated to his right represents profane love, love born from material well-being. Her left hand, which she has placed on the man's shoulder, and with her right-hand gesturing towards his lower body, indicate that she is influenced by her sexual polarity, however transitory, as the head wreath, she wears is not rooted therefore her dominion is of that the short-lived. Her long blue sleeves, slouching and open, indicate an inclination towards spirituality; but the blue hair reveals the superficiality in her. The sentimental effects caused by the attraction of material satisfactions cannot last, because it is nothing more than a simple mirage on the plane of physicality.

The woman situated to the left represents spiritual love and the love between the sexes in that most noble of states. Her hair, long and blonde, indicates the role of the sun and the inspirations that emanate from such love. Her left hand, she has placed on the man's chest showing that this superior love has the heart at its source. Her right hand[15] gesturing down emphasizing the ground, indicates that she causes matter to evolve. Her blue robe affirms her spiritual role and her dress edged in red, shows that she is adapting her sexuality towards spirituality. Her white arms determine the exaltation, she exerts on all levels by the harmonious synthesis in the range of feelings, which she is engendering.

The man personifies someone in a state of evolution in the whole of the cosmos, that is, all that is subject to love's laws of attraction. We symbolize this with a man, one representing the most elevated state, leading to highest spirituality. His tunic edged in red, shows the instinctive

---

[15] Translator: Please note, in the Emrik & Binger deck, this arm is yellow, indicating it belongs to the center figure, and not with the figure on the right, as implied in the Grimaud deck.

side of love, the blue, yellow and red stripes[16] highlights the various vibrations of love that filter through the different planes. The yellow of his arms and his hand[17] show the active tendencies, induced by intelligence towards divine love. His right hand on his belt, signifies that it is by a voluntary action that he has clearly separated spiritual love from visceral love. His hair, yellow, shows that intelligence needs to dominate and direct him in the physical plane. It is yellow, like the wreath on the woman to his right, it differs from it, in the sense that it represents an intelligence which is an integral part of man, and not just something transitory.

The yellow ground represents desires, stripped of feeling and reduced to the psyche, putting the evolutionary basis for this card in the realm of intelligence. The ground is wavy, thus indicating the oscillations of the instinct heading towards love.

ORIENTATION OF THE FIGURE

Cupid, turned a quarter to the right, prompts the evolutionary factors steering man, in whatever he does, towards his constant transformation, his unremitting evolution. The wreath wearing woman, whose profile is turned equally to the right, propels continuous action. The other whose head is turned to the left, while looking straight ahead, incites him to a life of the interior prior to a direct action. The man, facing ahead, with his head turned slightly to the left, is deciding on a choice after reflection.

---

[16] Translator: The card shown does not reflect Marteau´s text. The tunic is red, edged in yellow, not in 3 colours.

[17] Translator: Please note that the current Grimaud shows this hand in flesh colour. Older decks from Grimaud have depicted this hand in yellow. The Dusserre edition from Grimaud does however, depict this hand in yellow.

The ensemble represents therefore a complex one, with respect to action.

PARTICULAR AND CONCRETE MEANING

The intervention of sexual polarity in man in all activities, he is called forth to manifest, his action in the discernment that he is required to carry out, to direct his life, is what gives this card the name THE LOVER.

UTILITARIAN MEANINGS IN THE THREE PLANES

MENTAL. Love of beautiful forms in the arts of plasticity.

ANIMISTIC. Devotion and sacrifice.

PHYSICAL. Desires, love, sacrifice for one's country, similarly all strong feelings on the physical plane. A card of union, of marriage. It represents, for the querent of either gender, infidelity or, in certain cases, a choice to be made.

INVERTED. Disorder, division (as opposed to unifying), rupture, divorce.

*

In sum, in its elementary sense THE LOVER represents the sting of desire, which incites man to unite with the universal, whether harmoniously or in a state of imbalance, according to whether he sacrifices himself for it or in the want to derive profit from it.

THE CHARIOT
(Le Chariot)

PRINCIPLE

The number 7, as an odd number represents an activity, and by this number the 7 states of all things, such as the 7 notes on the musical scale, the 7 colours. It is represented in this card by 3 + 3 + 1; constituting the first

ternary, which is of a material order, consisting of the Chariot and the two horses, that is, by a mass with two dynamic poles. The second ternary, that of a spiritual order, is defined by the two shoulder masks and the man himself, who presents his two appearances as well as his realities. Finally, his means of action is the unity represented by his sceptre.

This will be explained further in the description of the card's attributes.

GENERAL AND ABSTRACT MEANING

This card represents THE SETTING IN MOTION IN THE SEVEN STATES, meaning, in all domains.

FEATURES BY ANALOGY

The Empress and the Emperor represent the two poles of power in the material world, to be understood in their own way, meaning, towards all action from their domains. The chariot is the physical vehicle of man, also an expression of material power, and more specifically, of action exercised by man on Earth, and so is symbolized by the figure depicted on this card.

It follows Arcanum VI, since love, when it exists as a divine spark, gives to man the power necessary for producing his manifestations in the material world.

The sceptre, crowned by a globe, a symbol of cosmic matter, manifests the power which man, once born, possess in the material plane.

The golden crown has the same regal significance, but, while the sceptre in his hand expresses the power of the law, the power of the crown represents the mental, fleeting as this can be. This power is exercised on the plane of cosmic matter, represented by the four elements, which are also indicated in the triangles, that make up his crown, comprising of four small spheres.

His blue, metallic cuirass states, that man in his ascendant and perilous movement forward through the material world, must be thoroughly dressed in spirituality in order to protect himself. It is white at the top, near the collar, and yellow below, because this spirituality must be directed by intelligence, which is of a divine nature and constitutes a part of this cuirass.

The stages of this movement forward, as well as the interior states which accompany them, are indicated by the

64

details engraved on the figure's cuirass. In fact, we can count fifteen points, divided into three series on the chevrons of the cuirass. The first two are comprised of six points each, making a total of 12, symbolising evolution. They form a polarization in where the upper and lower psyche, that is, the spiritual and the passions, are in opposition to one another and in this way, bring about each other's evolution.

The third chevron consists of three points representing what serves as the basis for the psyche of the 12 points. These are; the appetites, responding to the more primal aspects of man; the feelings, responding to his central and intimate aspects; the wants, responding to his higher aspects and mental aspects. The chevrons are isolated from one another to indicate that the points of the lower psyche, indicated in the bottom chevron, will not surpass their plane, which is of a purely physical order. These points represent the spiritual possibilities of man incarnated, possibilities that are limited on the physical plane. They cannot be extended into the abstract. However, the lower chevron does outline, by its position in the blue, a plane that allows the physical body to penetrate into the arcana of the psyche. The upper chevron manifests a different plane on which the spirit can rise high enough to surpass the arcana of physical life, entering the mental plane, and thus allow the spirit to escape from the body. In sum, these two upper chevrons indicate the two spiritual planes possible in the physical state.

The four points appearing on the yellow lower groin protection of the armour, represent the four states that are born from spirituality on the physical plane.[18]

The cuirass consists of three sections to show that, in accordance with his evolution, man is able to choose one

---

[18] Translator: Please note, the 1930 edition of the Grimaud deck depicts the Chariot with 9 points on the cuirass and the groin protection in white.

part of the breastplate and leave the other, or put on all three parts and assume complete possession of the spiritual protections, they bestow on him.

Under this cuirass, we find a red tunic, representing the material world which is necessary for man to overcome in order to evolve.

His right sleeve, being red, signifies that he here extracts active power from matter and from his left yellow sleeve, his passive states of intelligence. The red shoulder straps emerging from the mask on his left, symbolize the material world which his yellow arm must break off, expand with his intelligence.

The two masks covering his shoulders show the face of man incarnated, weighing on him as he is nothing but a transient creation. There are two of them: one created in the present and the other created from the past which he retrieves, but one is no more important than the other, as they are equal in size. They are red because they have been created by man's passions, and surrounded by yellow, as his intelligence lends them vigour, and so assigning them a momentary life. In other words, each man loses a face which his intelligence is able to rediscover or recreate with great accuracy, but this is of little importance over time.

This duality expressed by the two masks express man's internal and external face, the first one, the left mask, his mental aspect, the second the right mask, his side of action. The horizontal layout, a sign of passivity, places them in the intimate regions of man; and the pieces of fabric indicate, in addition to what has been mentioned, the fluid emanations of his psyche, fluids which penetrate the material world and so give the masks a point of support.

The figure's yellow hair sizes up the superior role of his intelligence.

The chariot symbolizes the currents, which lead man along and oblige him to act without cessation. It also

66

signifies that man is bounded by his own passions, entirely relative to him, as he is pulled and taken along with them. The pillars, by their spacing, show that he is able to escape towards what is above, and that he remains in his vehicle only by virtue of his passivity, which keeps him in the material world. Red in front and blue in the back, represents the equilibrium between the spiritual and material world, that which moves humanity forward.[19]

The flesh-coloured canopy – or the veil of physical life– him being beneath it, are the curtains off the heavens, but nonetheless easily removed, if one wishes.

The flesh-coloured wheels of the chariot, symbolize the cycles of life. The 12 nails visible on the wheel represent the 12 stages of evolution, through which man must travel in his life, as well as the 12 forms of temptation, which can test him on his path of evolution.

Spiritual activity, polarized in the material world, is represented by the red horse, the polarization of spirituality by the blue horse.[20]

The ground, yellow, indicates that man only advances by leaning on his understanding of the divine, and the tufts of green grass, are the images of hope, that are born with the progress of his advancement.

ORIENTATION OF THE FIGURE

The position of the figure, head on, indicates that his action needs to be directed, and by the heads of the two horses turned left, that intuition is necessary for progress.

---

[19] Translator: In the Grimaud, the coat of arms on the Chariot reads S.M. Most likely indicating Saul (Paul) Marteau, V.T. on this card is most likely referring to card maker Veuve Toulon.

[20] Translator: The card shown does not reflect Marteau´s text. Both horses are blue.

PARTICULAR AND CONCRETE MEANING

The name THE CHARIOT has been given to this card to indicate something tangible, of advancement, embodying an idea of embarkation and of progression. More generally, the material currents which pull man and oblige him to be in constant motion.

UTILITARIAN MEANINGS IN THE THREE PLANES

MENTAL. Achievements, but without gestation or inspiration. In other words, give shape.

ANIMISTIC. Display of affection, protector, beneficial, helpful.

PHYSICAL. Great activity, quick action. Good health, strength, hyperactivity. As it relates to money, expenditure, gain or transfer of funds. It signifies also unexpected news, conquest. It can be interpreted equally as propaganda by words and depending on where the card falls, good news or slander.

INVERTED. A bad card, indicating disorder in everything through negative activities, consequences of which are difficult to make up for. Accidents to fear. Bad news.

*

In short, in its elementary sense, THE CHARIOT represents the dangerous journey of man through the world of the material, to achieve spirituality, through the exercise of his powers and with the mastery of his passions.

68

THE JUSTICE
(La Justice)

PRINCIPLE

The number 8 can be broken down into (2 + 2) + (2 + 2) or 2 x 4. The first grouping implies a polarization of the number 4, that is, the quaternary viewed as active vs. passive and in its opposition, as spirit vs. matter. In other words, as the 4 is essentially material, it can be said 2 x 4 is 8 hence the developing material balance between the passivity of matter and the activity of same.

GENERAL AND ABSTRACT MEANING

This card is THE REPRESENTATION OF COSMIC INTELLIGENCE PENETRATING THE PLANE OF REALIZATIONS WITH THE AIM TO COORDINATE. This is why this card comes after the Chariot, in order to inspire humanity with the concept of

69

equilibrium and to regulate responsibilities and rights in its path of evolution.

FEATURES BY ANALOGY

The card shows a woman, whose feet are not visible, seated on a yellow throne, important and solid, because cosmic justice, proceeding from the divine, is immutable, dispassionate, and founded in intelligence. Her sword, held in her right hand and placed against the upper rail of the thrones back post, and with its pommel resting on her knee, indicates implacability, vigour, and rectitude. It is the sword posed to strike, resting on a base of justice, and with its yellow; representing sanctions applied with intelligence and without the spirit of vengeance.

The scales denote her capacity to make judgements in the material world; they are yellow along with the arm that supports them. The weighing is executed with intelligence.

Her head is completely covered by a yellow headdress. This spares her of the hotchpotch of thoughts on questions, she must pass judgement on, as well as detailing, that justice is completely boxed-in, meaning, it is isolated from all influence and encroachment, and that her intelligence is not her own, but form the intelligence of all those who come to the realization of what they are owed and what they owe. Her sovereignty is affirmed further by the golden crown completing her headdress, where the central circle in the shape of an eye, symbolizes her gaze, which man cannot escape, along with the fairness of her judgement.

The collar and the cord of gold together which she wears on top of her chest, show the portion of humanity, she brings into her judgement, while remaining bound to the laws of equilibrium.

Her red robe and her blue mantel represent the passionate activities on the plane of the psyche and on the physical plane which she wears in order to carry out her judgements.

The tufts of yellow grass indicate passive fertility, and the yellow earth is the foundation for wisdom.

ORIENTATION OF THE FIGURE

She is positioned head on, this is the only card that is presented in this way; it implies direct action to its fullest extent, but through inner work, given her seated position.

PARTICULAR AND CONCRETE MEANING

The title THE JUSTICE has been given to it, to represent the judgement of activities, which man has deployed for good or bad, in the course of his journey through the material world, as indicated by the previous cards.

UTILITARIAN MEANINGS IN THE THREE PLANES

MENTAL. Clarity of judgement, advice on fair assessments, knowing how to participate and appreciate eventualities.

ANIMISTIC. Dryness, contributing only with what is owed, possibility for cutting off emotional bonds, divorce, separation. This card constitutes the principle of rigor.

PHYSICAL. Trial, rehabilitation, justice rendered. Balance of health, but with surplus, owing to the immobility of the card.

INVERTED. Loss, condemnation, injustice, trial with conviction. Great disorder, people victimized by underhanded people.

*

In short, in its elementary sense, THE JUSTICE represents the judgment imposed on man by his deep awareness, in order to appreciate the balance and imbalance engendered by his actions, with all their happy and painful consequences.

THE HERMIT
(L'Hermite)

PRINCIPLE

The number 9 = 3 x 3, that is, three secondary ternaries included in one general ternary. These ternaries correspond to the three cosmic planes, which can be interpreted to be; the physical, the spiritual, and the mental, or by the terms; life, love, and light.

The secondary ternaries are reflections of each element in the first ternary; they are clothed by them, but yet still separated from them. Therefore, love embraces life and light, and light is love and life. Without life, love does not manifest, and without light, it cannot be illuminated. Likewise, the spiritual exhibits a physical and mental quality; without the physical, the spirit could not be made concrete, without the mental, it would remain incoherent and devoid of all restrictions.

The grouping of this ternary, in the number 9, suggests a perfect coordination of all these elements.

73

GENERAL AND ABSTRACT MEANING

This card represents WISDOM REFRACTING IN MATTER, wisdom in where truth is found, deeply veiled and hidden from human eyes. It is love and light, entering into the matters of life.

FEATURES BY ANALOGY

This card follows The Justice searching for the truth, indispensable for rendering justice.

The lantern, alternating between yellow and red, which the Hermit holds in his right hand, indicates that his search must be carried out as much in the domain of light as in that of the spiritual. The top of the lantern, entirely yellow, shows that this search is guided by intelligence. It is in opposition to his robe and mantel, since it does not need to be sharply illuminated. As light cannot be found without personal reflection, the robe clothing him is that symbol. It is blue, with yellow lining, because spirituality must be internally intelligent. The one who seeks it without intelligence does not find it. The yellow lining which can be found on a corner of the mantel, to the left of the Hermit, is there to indicate that this intelligence is not so concealed, that man cannot see it, for he needs it to evolve.

The red robe under the blue mantel shows that man remains ever impregnated with matter and that it is in matter that he must find the truth. This interior garment represents, therefore, an inescapable material state, with which we are obliged to clothe ourselves, while the mantel is the garment, which we choose to clothe ourselves, according to our purpose and state of evolution.

The red hood signifies, that truth appears to be intimately entangled with matter, always in a relationship with intelligence. The yellow ball on the tip, shows that intelligence always wins in the end, whatever the situation may be. In other words, this hood symbolizes momentary states of matter, which one is able to throw off quickly, if one wants to.

The staff, flesh coloured, touching the ground indicates the connection, which man is able to establish with the physical plane through his vital fluids. It signifies likewise that his path is hard to climb and that man frequently needs help, which he will receive from the physical world.

The Hermit's hair and beard are flesh coloured, since he evolves through the receptive and active play of his fluids.

The yellow lantern, grooved in parallel lines, shows that he must always orient himself to the same ends, that of divine initiation.

ORIENTATION OF THE FIGURE

He is standing in profile, with his head turned mostly forward. He is with his thoughts, oriented towards direct action in reflection. The nature of his walk, is calm and reflective, and his stance suggests work with purpose.

PARTICULAR AND CONCRETE MEANING

The name THE HERMIT is given to this card to represent man´s retreat into himself to examine the results of the actions, which Justice has sanctioned.

UTILITARIAN MEANINGS IN THE THREE PLANES

MENTAL. A source of illumination and resolve to some problem. A clarity which will appear spontaneous.

ANIMISTIC. A source of solution. Coordination, aligning with affinity. This signifies prudence as well, not from the perspective of fear but through improvement.

PHYSICAL. A secret unveiled, a light which will be shed on hidden affairs. With respect to health: a source of knowledge about the state of one's health with advice on its cure.

INVERTED. Obscurity, faulty understanding of a situation, the difficulty of going against the current.

*

In sum, in its elementary sense, THE HERMIT represents man in his search for truth, calmly and patiently, using logic and light, partly in secret, which he directs with prudence.

THE WHEEL OF FORTUNE
(La Roue de Fortune)[21]

PRINCIPLE

The number 10, within its context, is formed by the unity following the zero, symbolizing a departure and an accomplishment, and consequently an evolution.

GENERAL AND ABSTRACT MEANING

This card represents THE PREPARATION OF MAN FOR A NEW CYCLE, ONE RESULTING FROM A PRECEDING CYCLE. It is the law of destiny and comes after card VIIII because truth and knowledge are at the foundation of this evolution.

---

[21] Translator: *La Roue de Fortune* and not *La Roue de la Fortune* in French would imply a translation that reads; Fortune´s Wheel. However, the name The Wheel of Fortune has become the predominant translation for this card in English.

FEATURES BY ANALOGY

This card presents three phases, as indicated by the three animal figures on the card, in order to show that they apply to all beings of creation.

The first phase, a monkey on the descent, represents a descending evolution, a phase of instinct, which is not guided by intelligence, but by cunning or by skill, the full adaptation to physical life. It corresponds to involution, that is, the descent of divine spark onto matter, this association is symbolized by the colour flesh. The animal lifts its head in dislike, as the descend is involuntary. Its red and blue costume indicates an instinctive adaptation with the cosmos, manifested both in the material as well as in the spiritual plane. It separates the superior parts of the animal from the inferior, in the sense, that the inferior parts, more attached to the soil, must pass away for it to evolve.

The second phase, the dog[22] represents the first degree of ascendance, the first flash of intelligence, which is why it is yellow. Its head, turned up, shows the germ of the beginnings of human emotions. Its vest, blue, skirt red, signifies that its intelligence is beginning to perceive the rudiments of spirituality and the need to leave matter behind. Its claws indicate that desires are still exerted, the dog collar, that it is still a slave, and even in this moment of self-liberation, attentively perceived with its ears. Its green[23] colour represents scientific adaptation, which is beginning to manifest in this second phase of its evolution.

The third phase, the third figure, in shape of a sphinx, indicates destiny, unknown to man in his path of evolution,

---

[22] Translator: Please note, that many believe this animal represents the donkey or the mule, not the dog, since the donkey in times past, was seen as a particularly useful and productive animal.

[23] Translator: Please note, in the current Grimaud deck there is no green on the ears. Older decks from Grimaud, have been depicted with green on the collar though.

78

his aspirations towards an unknown, which he must decipher. This is the mystery to be unveiled, the last stage, that he, however, is obligated to pass, but the sphinx, will not answer the question, asked of him, about this ultimate goal. Man continues to enter into and out of matter, to return anew and to leave again through his successive lives, until man finds, on his own, an answer to his question.

The sphinx is the manifestation of the role of the divine in evolution. Its crown of gold represents its supreme royal authority, the certainty of its judgement. Its sword is inescapable justice. This, held in its left hand, indicates its passivity, and the white blade expresses its neutrality. Its red wings show that divinity, of which the sphinx is an expression of, is in all things, and it having interpreted the world of matter, must escape it, without delay. Its body is blue, because it is the representation of pure and essential spirituality. The platform on which it rests is yellow, characterizing divine intelligence.

The two yellow posts, supporting the wheel are the two poles of intelligence, active and passive, between which evolution must take place. They in turn rest on beams on the ground, also yellow, and connected with two crossbeams, in order to emphasize the solidity and immutability of its foundation.

The wheel represents the cosmos; its drive wheel is flesh-coloured, lines in black. This deals with the role of the cosmos on the physical plane. The centre hub is red, because the two poles, in order to spin, must act before anything else on the material plane, then by the blue spokes, on the spiritual plane, and, from there, through the white spokes, on the mental plane. This last is represented by the colour white, not yellow, because it is detached from the intelligence owing to physical life. This separation in the form of the blue joint-rings represents the barrier, often impassable, which separates the spiritual from the higher mind. When man breaks through this barrier, he ceases to go on having successive lives.

The spokes of the wheel, being similar in essence, represent a link between the interior and external life. Their number indicates the six planes of evolution, that is, starting from the lowest vibration ending with the highest: The Physical, the Animistic, the Mental, the Causal, the Spiritual, and the Divine. There are six spokes and not seven, since a seventh plane would symbolize a final destination and would deviate from the card's correct meaning, which is to point out the steps of evolution.

The crank indicates that man is able to slow down or speed up his own evolution. It symbolizes his capacity for free will, and indicates that he is not a slave to his destiny. He decides by the colour white how neutral his power will be.

The ground, flesh coloured, grooved, represents the pivots of the poles in their mode of subtle resistance, on the physical plane. The flesh coloured rods joining the two supporting beams at the foundation of the wheel, represent the currents of life on the physical plane, but are bound inseparably to the mental plane, representing thus both involution and evolution.

ORIENTATION OF THE FIGURE

The different position of each, makes this a complicated card. The sphinx is still and facing forward, the dog is in profile and ascending, likewise the monkey is in profile but descending. In as much, it is the sphinx who commands, and allows the action, one of the animals is active in its ascend, the other is passive as it descends, however the wheel turns regardless, so luck alternates and substitutes between the two, in their path of evolution.

PARTICULAR AND CONCRETE MEANING

The name THE WHEEL OF FORTUNE has been given to it, because the movement of the wheel implies a cycle, that returns to its point of origin, but brings with it the experiences acquired during its path. Experiences which will result in favourable or dire circumstances.

UTILITARIAN MEANINGS IN THE THREE PLANES

MENTAL. Logic, as the wheel evokes balance and regularity. Sound and balanced judgement.

ANIMISTIC. Participation, vitality, and strengthening of feelings.

PHYSICAL. Whatever the events that occur in the querent's life, they are not stable, they are moving towards an evolution, a change, necessarily happy in nature, because the card is not a reversed. Security while in doubt. From the point of view of health: Good circulation. For married couples: fulfilling activities.

INVERTED. The transformation will be done with difficulty, but it will be done regardless. It is not nefarious, but causes delays, due to current circumstances. It indicates that there is change in foundations and new beginnings.

*

In sum, in its elementary sense, THE WHEEL OF FORTUNE represents man in the midst of present actions, which have their origin in cyclical work of the past and which prepare for those to come in future, on which the divine in the end will award, whatever their vicissitudes.

THE STRENGTH
(La Force)

PRINCIPLE

The number 11 is equal to 10 + 1, meaning, a principle of departure, 1 resuming after a cycle of 10, which the Wheel of Fortune has examined. This principle, made up by the knowledge, that has been acquired in this cycle, thus represents a force, which does not come from up high, but which appears as an accumulated energy.

GENERAL AND ABSTRACT MEANING

This card represents the powers which result from completing a cycle. It indicates, consequently, struggles and the will to win, a state which can only be realized if man masters this force, rather than it mastering him. This will of the spirit is symbolized by a woman, in order to show that force should be exercised without violence.

FEATURES BY ANALOGY

Her hat, blue, yellow, and white[24], represents the three states of consciousness; spirituality, intelligence, and superior mentality. The dress´ braided section indicates the link between the spiritual and the mental. The algebraic symbol in the shape of the infinity sign ∞, which has no beginning nor end, means that it embraces the entire universe, and that it ensures its strength through equilibrium. This is the will of beings on all planes.

The black line around her neck represents the demarcation, between a higher intelligent physical plane and a lower physical plane, which is subordinate to intelligence.

The blue dress and the yellow corset, with tight lacing, show that the spiritual is a state in her, surrounded by intelligence, and the mantle reduced to a red drop fold and not wrapped around the body, is exerting its action into material activities, in which, she cannot secure a victory, of more than a fleeting and disappointing nature.

The arm that symbolizes the act of force, is dressed up with pleated yellow sleeves, and flesh-coloured cuffs, thus indicating that its actions, guided by human intelligence, operate in the plane of physical life, as much as outside of it, meaning, in incarnated beings as well as in disincarnated beings. For this reason, her foot is bare, and appears under her dress, specifying that victories are found in advance, and that this forward march can be done on any plane.

The yellow lion represents the intelligent force of nature, against which man must fight, under threat of being

---

[24] Translator: Please note, the card shown does not reflect Marteau´s text. The hat is blue, yellow and red, not blue yellow and white.

devoured by it. She separates the lion's jaws, thus demonstrating that she must look inside, in order to take on the forces hidden within, to know and to subdue them. This lion is also a representation of divine's intelligence and the immutable force, that exists in the cosmos and in man, inseparable, because it is in opposition to power, albeit half hidden and without an aggressive demeanour, as if it were a part of it. No force can have effective action, without a close union between man, the cosmos and the divine.

ORIENTATION OF THE FIGURE

Strength keeps her head facing forward, however turned slightly to the right. The position of the head, leaning to the left, indicates thought and reflection. It is oriented towards an action, but must take time before carrying it out. Her body, not being entirely turned to the right, ultimately means that she is leaving reflection to move towards an effective action.

PARTICULAR AND CONCRETE MEANING

The name of the card, THE STRENGTH, specifies that this in a sense is, personal force over matter.

UTILITARIAN MEANINGS IN THE THREE PLANES

MENTAL. It gives great power to recognize truth from what is false, the useful from the useless, and unmistakable judgements.

ANIMISTIC. In control of passions, the power of conquest. Example: A woman to be married will draw strength from affection. Affectionate protection.

PHYSICAL. The will to overcome conflicts and to master a situation, since one is one the side of right. The power to lead in all material matters.

INVERTED. Man is no longer the master of his strength; he is brutal, immoral, or gets carried away, does not use it. Conflicts or people will get the best of him, his strength will be annihilated and he will be the victim of higher powers.

*

In sum, in its elementary sense, THE STRENGTH represents the powers available to man, the fruits of his efforts, which he is able to exercise in all planes, when he does so in accordance with divine laws.

THE HANGED MAN
(Le Pendu)

PRINCIPLE

While the number 10 represents a natural periodic cycle, like the days, the months, or the years, the number 12 represents a cycle completed, but not in the process of renewal, as a change is needed in the principle, which formed the foundation of the cycle, to begin with. Therefore, the number 12 implies, a renunciation, so a new cycle can start, if there is one, and if not obstructed by the work of the preceding cycle, and if it can be reoriented towards a new path. This is why this card is not directly related to the Strength card, but rather to the entire preceding series of cards, because it completes the primary cycle of the Tarot, that of 12. The 22 Tarot Major Arcana are, in effect, formed by the two cycles 12 + 10.

One could consider the 22 cards making up the grouping; 3 x 7 + 1, but this interpretation, which does not stand up to theoretical rigor, represents only an inferior aspect of the Tarot, subordinated to the ternary (3 x 7), which follows the principle of beginnings (1), without the continuation. It is instead the passive will of man (2), facing an actively self-serving organization (10).

GENERAL AND ABSTRACT MEANING

This card signifies A HALT OR SUSPENSION IN THE EVOLUTIONARY WORK OF MAN.
The representation of this suspension, by an inverted man, indicates, that the man who is elevated, is like the man who is down, and that all acts of man on the material plane are reflected on the spiritual plane. Implying, that man pulls the spiritual towards the material, and vice-versa, in the end to allow the union of these two aspects of the cosmos.

FEATURES BY ANALOGY

The blue shoes on the hanged man indicate, that man is clothed in spirituality, even though he is immersed in matter, the red legs, which are the acts of the lower material, held up high. His blue jacket and yellow skirt means, that the man plunges the spiritual into matter, since the head, that is, the upper part of himself, is at the bottom on this card, doing so with intelligence and a spirit of sacrifice. This is why his hands are tied behind his back, showing, proving, that this return to matter is voluntary and that he accepts his destiny. His buttoned jacket reveals, that he is voluntarily held in this state of sacrifice. The 9 buttons, that secure this enclosure along with their white seam, form a polarization, represented by the skirt. These

87

together are the three divine states, and so the jacket, becomes the 10 phases of evolution, that lead man to renunciation. The seam is white to indicate that this is decided in a spirit of spiritual synthesis.

This sacrifice must be made without a calculated reward. This is why the hands are hidden and the pockets unusable, man stuck in the physical world of the reverse. It shows that all material wealth acquired in the physical plane does not remain. The white belt indicates the separation of the animistic from the mental (yellow skirt), as well as, the deciding role played by the latter, which, being upside down, is above the spiritual (blue jacket).

The arms, flesh-coloured with red sleeves, reinforce the ties that unite man with passion and vitality; but his blue hair indicates, that spirituality still remains deep within him. The green ground, on which the trees stand, indicate, on one hand, that the sacrifice is a rich seed, it bears its fruits, and, on the other, that intellectual knowledge also guides man towards his evolution.

The two trees that support the Hanged Man, represent the trees of life, forming with the horizontal green branch on top a portico, which encloses the man and forces him to a continuously repeat his struggles. The duality of the trees recall the polarization of the masculine and feminine. They are yellow because the intellectual knowledge of man, always elevates him towards deep and divine intelligence, and the six branches cut, in red, indicate the six stages, that the two poles of humanity, must experience, in order to evolve in matter.

Man is suspended from a green branch, because he is frequently detained in scientific pursuits. The rope is white, neutral, because man can only tie himself by his will. He does so, on one hand, in the spiritual plane, by his foot, from the physical plane; his hands, that is, by the spirit of sacrifice, the result; he remains tied up. However, it is shown by his leg, which is bent and free, that he can still break free. In the example of the case of a very religious man, stuck in his beliefs, and so, as a consequence slowed in his evolution, unable to advance.

ORIENTATION OF THE FIGURE

The position of the Hanged Man symbolizes latent activity.

PARTICULAR AND CONCRETE MEANING

The name THE HANGED MAN symbolizes a halt in preparation for a transition, a transformation, a path from the concrete to the abstract, and consequently a state of no-response, a blocking of the power to act.

UTILITARIAN MEANINGS IN THE THREE PLANES

MENTAL. A very diverse set of possibilities, reminiscence of the past, of the present, and of the future, of decision making, resulting in hesitation. This card indicates things of insufficient maturation of no conclusion.

ANIMISTIC. A lack of determination, of indecision, specifically in affective choice.

PHYSICAL. Forsaking something, renunciation, doubtful affairs. Momentary impotence in power of action. If some business were to be undertaken, it would remain a dream and not brought into realization, without assistance. With respect to health; circulatory problems owing to lack of harmony resulting from the position of the hooked foot.

INVERTED. Exit possible, but uneven, in affairs quite sentimental, unsatisfying and without pleasure, because the circumstances of the Hanged Man found standing, but in a state of imbalance and with his hands tied behind his back. Reluctance and secret affairs.

*

In sum, in its elementary sense, THE HANGED MAN represents, man subverting his action, to orient himself towards the spiritual, in the feeling of hesitation and renunciation.

DEATH
(Le Mort)

PRINCIPLE

The number 13 is equal to 12 + 1. It symbolizes the beginning of a new cycle, in the general evolution embodied by the tarot. This card is related to the Hanged Man, as it pertains to having an account of the knowledge acquired by the preceding cycle, from which man must remove, what may be useless or harmful, which does not suit the nature of the new cycle. Also, because of the spirit of sacrifice, implied by the Hanged Man, leading to the light, whose doors open with the disappearance of the physical body. This card is about the activity that intervenes in a preserved state of things.

GENERAL AND ABSTRACT MEANING

This Arcanum means; TRANSFORMATION, SYMBO-LIZING THE MOVEMENT, THE PASSAGE, FROM ONE PLANE OF LIFE TO ANOTHER PLANE OF LIFE. It is in the invisible plane, the opposition to God´s image in our world, representing, in effect, immobility in physical life and the march into the hereafter.

FEATURES BY ANALOGY

The colour of flesh on the skeleton indicates, the persistence of human individuality, thus underlining that this is not just about a physical death but that another form of life remains in man.

The abandonment of all terrestrial attributes is symbolized by the stripping of flesh and clothing, conserving only the necessary framework for the new to envelope. The principle of life, which the colour of the skeletons symbolizes, show the transformation, that it imposes and without which, man would remain stagnant, thus carrying out a real death.

The skeleton is reaping in a black space, which symbolizes the dark passions of men, as well as the new evolutionary path, still shrouded in darkness. His hands and feet are not cut off, but represent a principle of action and progression. They mean that death frees man from his physical life, leaving with him the gesture and the advance. Indeed, the advance, is indicated by the foot planted flat, showing that man advances from one incarnation to another; the gesture, indicated by the hand, a symbol of touch and sensitivity, also placed flat, is what makes it to the next incarnation. They are in black soil to indicate that, despite of death, man is linked to the earth and that death takes its point of support on it and in it, so that he can be reborn. The two hands that protrude from the black soil show that death incites man to detach himself from matter and to elevate his gestures to the above. The two white bones represent the emptiness of the material, the two polarities of male and female. The head of the long-haired child indicates, that strength and intelligence survive death, likewise that divine intelligence is always found in man in a childlike state.[25] The crowned head means, every time death occurs, man enters his kingdom. The head is an adult, the royalty of men, it is an immutable thing, it has neither childhood nor old age.

Yellow and blue leaves symbolize fertility; death cannot cut them down. They flourish every time man crosses the path of death. This fertility comes both from the knowledge acquired on the physical plane, and from the forces of evolution belonging to the spiritual plane.

The handle on the scythe is yellow, because death comes from a divine and intelligent will, and the scythe blade is red, because death always cuts in the world of matter. Moreover, the scythe is not, in this card, a representation of a cutting instrument, but rather the symbol of an activity, that arms the material in order to renew it and make it available again.

The skeleton has only one foot to indicate, that death implies a disequilibrium and can only act on the physical plane and not on the spiritual. It is not an aspect of harmony, but of consequence.

ORIENTATION OF THE FIGURE

The figure´s profile, entirely towards the right, indicates transition, renewal, successive actions, with the indication of advancement; transformations with every step.

---

[25] Translator: "*toujours en l´homme a l´etat d´enfance*", perhaps Marteau here is referring to Carl Jung´s discovery of the soul "Self". Jung has been known to have described this as;" God in my soul is a child".

93

PARTICULAR AND CONCRETE MEANING

Contrary to the other cards, it has no name assigned, although its image traditionally represents that of death. Since death does not exist, it cannot be named, because it would give this card a pejorative meaning, that it does not have. Its authentic meaning is that of transmutation, but this word, in itself, cannot be chosen either, because transmutation is at the origin of life and this origin is beyond words.

UTILITARIAN MEANINGS IN THE THREE PLANES

MENTAL. Renewal of ideas, completely or in part, because something is going to intervene and transform everything, like a catalytic phenomenon, where a new body completely modifies the actions of the bodies that are in its presence.

ANIMISTIC. Estrangement, scattering of affection, the wear and tear of a feeling, of hope.

PHYSICAL. Death, the ending of something, immobility. In the matter of business; complete transformation.

INVERTED. From the point of view of health; stagnation, death can be avoided, but the condition is incurable. In its surroundings, it indicates death, and of implications persisting beyond the death itself.

*

In sum, in its elementary sense, Arcanum XIII represents the change of states of consciousness in man, which accompanies the completion of a cycle and is at the beginning of a naturally different type of cycle.

94

TEMPERANCE
(Tempérance)

PRINCIPLE

The number 14 is equal to 12 + 2, meaning, to an accompanying evolutionary period, enclosed in a polarity. This is why this card takes its power from a concentration, due to the experience of a completed cycle, that works in a closed circuit, generating a movement between two soft, passive reservoirs, which compress one another.

GENERAL AND ABSTRACT MEANING

This card symbolizes THE GREAT RESERVOIR OF POSSIBILITIES THROUGH THE ETERNAL PLAY OF THE ENERGIES OF MATTER, it represents the eternal resumption. It follows card XIII, because this card does not mark an end.

FEATURES BY ANALOGY

The figure is that of an angel, in order to give meaning to immateriality, to show that her action is not the fruit from the work of men. She has blue hair, a sign of spirituality. The red star on her forehead guides her and shows that she can only act in the physical plane. Her flesh-coloured wings underline this action in the vital plane.

The red arms show the interpenetration into the physical plane, the dress with various colours make her particularly intellectual and spiritual, with which she covers herself to hide the divine. Her work is carried out only in the world of energies.

The dress is half red, half blue, because this balance must be maintained both in spirituality and in the material world, which cannot be separated.

The angel leans to show, that it is the blue pitcher of physical spirituality, she pours into the red pitcher of matter. Her gesture and her position are persistent; while she remains upright, she can lean towards either side.

The two pitchers symbolize the perpetual renewal that establishes the balance between materiality and spirituality, eternally pouring one into the other, without ever filling, forever renewing matter. The colourless water, neutral, represents the fluid, that joins the two poles, and in fact, are neutralized, starting from the blue pitcher and returning to same, following the principle of flow and ebb of forces.

The angel is posing on yellow ground with green plants, to show that she has a divine basis with her action in the material, a basis that produces a terrestrial, but not divine, flowering.

ORIENTATION OF THE FIGURE

Her body is facing the front, but her head is turned to the left, indicating that she takes her time to reflect, because necessary time is needed, in reconciling the extremes of Temperance, before an action can be effective.

PARTICULAR AND CONCRETE MEANING

The title TEMPERANCE has been given to her, because she acts as a conciliator in all things.

UTILITARIAN MEANINGS IN THE THREE PLANES

MENTAL. It brings the spirit of conciliation. The absence of passion in a trial. It provides deep meaning to things, representing an eternal principle, a psychic personality, not imposing an idea of stability, but something rather plastic, that is, moving, adapting to circumstances.

ANIMISTIC. People brought together by kinship; under the influence of this card they are satisfied, but they do not evolve and they do not leave the relationship.

PHYSICAL. In business, conciliation, the pros and cons are weighed, compromises are found, but it is unknown, whether the enterprise will be successful. Reflection, a decision that is not taken right away. From the point of view of health; incurable disease, because it engenders its own fermentation.

INVERTED. Upset, disagreements, but misrepresentation and hesitation will be overturned.

*

In sum, in its elementary sense, TEMPERANCE represents the work of adapting to a new activity, the work of kneading, which man performs in order to readjust to the new, and in a more broader sense, material energies readjusting to spiritual energies.

THE DEVIL
(Le Diable)

PRINCIPLE

Among the different combinations, that make up the number 15, the arrangement 10 + 5 = 15, and 11 + 4 = 15, are particularly suited for the context of card XV. It is man introducing his particular vibration into an organized

grouping. This activity takes place in opposition to the universal rhythm; thus, he is represented by the Devil.

10 means a completed cycle. 5 = 4 + 1 indicates a repetition of the cycle, an activity which penetrates the material world, that arises to work against it and to give to it, through vibration, the rhythm of life, represented by 5. From a different point of view, 10 represents the equilibrium of a completed cycle and 5 marks the instability of a new risky beginning. 11 indicates force and 4 matter; therefore, 11 + 4 = 15, signifying the force of will, energetically stroking

99

matter and able to be used for good as well as for evil. This combination confirms and accentuates the previous, the one obtained by means of 10 + 5, and this is why this card follows Temperance who has the ability to materialize. The eternal repetitions of Temperance is done on the moral plane, unlike the Devil, who takes it onto the human plane.

GENERAL AND ABSTRACT MEANING

The Devil represents; A PRINCIPLE OF SPIRITUAL ACTIVITY THAT TRIES TO PENETRATE MATTER AND CLOTHE ITSELF IN IT, IN ORDER TO MATERIALIZE. He symbolizes a great evolution, because although he is the symbol of evil, he is also that of triumph. It is men who have conferred the symbol of maleficence onto it, it is deep, of divine essence and as necessary to humanity, as good is, constituting a bridge between good and evil, divinity, as man understands it, and can be viewed, depending on its interpretation, as good or evil.

FEATURES BY ANALOGY

His headdress is a crown of flames, to show that his origin takes place on a higher plane, because the Devil actually expresses the work of man in the universe, with the support of the divine, he himself therefore does not cease to be an expression of the divine laws.

His blue wings, directed upwards, show that his action tends to produce an evolution upward. His torch frames the world of illusion, its white flame indicates his neutrality, and men, according to what activity they attribute to him in his domain, will give it colour.

The torso bare, showing breasts and male genitalia at the same time, represents the male and female fertility in the vital forces of nature. His right arm is raised to affirm

100

that his action comes from above, but his flesh-coloured claws and his position on terrain of the same colour, that he is trapped in the material plane, and that he will never be able to act on a divine plane. His red belt denotes that he is entirely surrounded by matter, even in its lowest expressions. His blue legs show that he makes man evolve towards spirituality.

His hermaphroditism, indicated by the simultaneous representation of the attributes of both sexes, show, depending on, whether it is situated from the universal point of view, or from a particular point of view, that he perpetually engenders the renewal of matter by himself, penetrating it, with his vital force, or drawing everything back to him, because, by capturing the two, male and female poles in himself, he works in a closed circuit and captures these vital forces for himself.

His red pedestal indicates that he dominates the material world. Its dimensions are modest, to show that his kingdom is precarious and has been made unstable by his nefarious activities. The two beings tied to the pedestal are the emanations of the Devil and represent the exterior of his sexual polarity, showing that man is chained and that he will suffer the consequences in exchange for its rewards, without the ability for escape. The two beings symbolize, consequently for the whole world, the experience of being dominated in human and animal matter, of being slaves. They are masculine and feminine because they extend the two principles of polarity to the world. They have red bands on their heads, to indicate that man can mentally trap himself in the material, the Devil himself, not a representative of any principles of elevation. The black flames, the ears and the tails of animals, indicate that the Devil is a necessary force in evolution. A force from which one must emancipate oneself and without this effort, man embedded in the material cannot progress. Gloomy emanations, indeed. In other words, the Devil symbolizes man chained by nature, which stirs up an animal in him.

This chain has its origin in the laws of cause and effect; meaning, in the consequences produced by man's past actions. The effects are bad, when man lets himself be chained by matter, and evolutionary, when he makes an effort to get rid of them.

The ground, wild, with black stripes on a yellow background, means that the emanations of matter turned into evil can hide the source of divine intelligence. The parallelism of the lines indicates that the two walk together.

ORIENTATION OF THE FIGURE

The main figure is faced forward, suggesting a direct act of domination, by contrast the smaller figures are a quarter turned: the one on the left (the female) towards the right, and the one on the right (the masculine) towards the left, with their heads almost faced forward, hence in opposite directions, in so suggesting the force of passivity combined with that of activity – but with constraints and disharmony as designated by their attachments, their horns, and other animal features.

PARTICULAR AND CONCRETE MEANING

The name THE DEVIL has been given to this card because it represents man acting in the material world through his own power, without spiritual support, so that when he is not in search of spirituality, he is subject to the temptations of transgressing against cosmic morality and capitulating to his instincts. The card signifies, therefore, success in the material world through direct effort and through the council of reason, or the surrender to the inevitable.

UTILITARIAN MEANINGS IN THE THREE PLANES

MENTAL. Great selfish activity without concern for justice, this card does not have a practical significance on the spiritual plane.

ANIMISTIC. Plurality, diversity, inconsistency, because it is sought with all senses and brought back to oneself only, without concern for others. Debauchery.

PHYSICAL. Great radiation on this plane, particularly in the material domain, in concrete achievements. Great ability to influence others. This is, however, a physically deficient card; this success is obtained through the bad arts. Consequently, fortune acquired in a reprehensible way, or by theft that has gone unpunished. In the affective domain, it is the conquest of man by reprehensible practices, without scruples, involving the destruction of other men, but having success regardless. For this reason, it is a card announcing punishment, because, when appearing in a spread, it announces that the triumph will only be momentary, followed by its lessons, if the question posed is not exempt from selfishness. As a disease, it indicates great nervous instability, symbolized by the claws that attract fluids, from control and possession, consequences from the past.

INVERTED. Its actions have a very bad foundation, with even more evil results. Disorder, inversion, shady deals or deals without results. From the point of view of health, increase of sickness, complications.

*

In sum, in its elementary sense THE DEVIL represents a form of human activity, the stirring up of matter, of which man will become a slave, after having achieved a temporary success, or will free himself, with the powers of knowledge, according to weather his goals are selfish or that of material evolution.

THE TOWER
(La Maison-Dieu)

PRINCIPLE

The number 16 can be presented in the form of 10 + 6. 10 represents a completed cycle, but which is renewed indefinitely, therefore a universal cycle, and 6 symbolizes involution and evolution, rise and fall, ephemeral construction and of starting again. 10 + 6 = 16 manifests the power of man, who wants to undertake everything, but who, being limited, cannot reach permanence; the fatally unstable construction.

GENERAL AND ABSTRACT MEANING

The tower shows THE LIMIT OF HUMAN POWER AND ITS IMPOSSIBILITY IN PERMANENT CONSTRUCTIONS.

The preceding card, the Devil meant, among other things, evil, but evil being a human interpretation, therefore does not really exist. There are only forces that struggle for progress. The Tower comes after the Devil, because it represents human progress, which consists in a perpetual rebuilding, of what will always be demolished, the very principle of progress.

Therefore, the tower means that every construction, created by man is destined to be destroyed, be it a mental construction or a physical construction, because everything that takes its foundation in matter will disappear.

FEATURES BY ANALOGY

The tower symbolizes a defective, erroneous construction, in which man encloses himself with self-deception. It is flesh-coloured, because it is built in the midst of the vital energies of man on the physical plane.

The windows are blue; the wise man, who builds his tower, must always keep an eye toward spirituality. The yellow rampart means, that man always wishes to crown and deliver his work with a stamp of intelligence, however a purely human intelligence and so without efficacy. Fire destroys the works of man; but the yellow colour of the flames, as with the ground, signify, that they will be purified in returning to the earth, on whose contact, natural vital energies is provided, giving them the ability to start over.

In other words, fire is the force, that man can always draw from, the divine, to continue his work, which is never finished. It also represents the purifying flame, that man will pass through, when he leaves his transitory building, passing on to the divine plane. The flame, by its red colour, also indicates his action in matter and, by its yellow colour, his divine intelligence. The blue and red man, who falls touching the ground with his hands, shows that whatever

106

the cause that has made him fall - matter or spirituality – he will take up the fluidic forces from the earth again, supporting his hands on the ground and restart his task. His pose in a semicircle, evokes the image of the outstretched hand by which, man performs his actions on the outside world, he symbolizes the active pole. Thus, it describes the man who has operated on the environment, who has played his constructive combinations and who has subsequently failed.

The second figure, whose sense of fall is opposite to that of the first, and whose pose seems horizontal, symbolizes the second pole, the passive pole, and his fall is heavier, because man who, by inertia, is unable to control the forces of that, he has taken over, loses the support, that was given to them and he falls back on to matter. His fall is not the direct result of his actions, but a slow descent produced by distant causes.

The balls are the seeds of this construction, falling on the earth to germinate again. The red and blue, mean that the reconstructions will be material or spiritual, the white balls represent the apparent futility of the effort. None are yellow, because divine intelligence does not preside over this card, which applies exclusively to the work of man. They represent, by their number, the multiple forms on which man can build on the physical plane. This is about the various contributions from men on different levels.

The soil, yellow[26] with sprouts of green, indicates fertilized human labour bears fruit.

ORIENTATION OF THE FIGURE

The position of the tower is frontal, indicating a direct, violent action.

---

[26] Translator: The card shown does not reflect Marteau´s text. The ground is flesh-coloured, not yellow.

SPECIFIC AND CONCRETE SENSE

The name of this card, THE TOWER (LA MAISON-DIEU[27]) comes from the fact that God, being omnipresent, is also in the buildings man constructs. But as he does not intervene and man is in the dark, his constructions are imperfect and destined for destruction. These constructs born in the thoughts of man, and according to him, strongly built, are devoured by the same flame that fuels his desires, and thus cause their fall. The tower, made of dense materials, is too concrete to allow for, the subtlety of the spiritual currents, represented by the lightning bolt. It disintegrates.

The tower also means that man, believing himself almighty, erects it to extend his dominion, but since his free will is very limited, he sees it collapse, when he believes it to be permanent, and then he must begin again. It also symbolizes man trapped in his ideas and founding theories, which vanish with experience.

UTILITARIAN MEANINGS IN THE THREE PLANES

MENTAL. Indication of the danger of continuing in a certain path, with a fixed idea, and a warning in order to avoid the consequences, under pain of violent turmoil and annihilation.

ANIMISTIC. Domination by man, without charity or love, exerted on others with despotism, and which sooner or later, will be rejected out of affection.

---

[27] Translator: *La Maison Dieu* translated directly would read; *God's House*, however the predominant translation for this card in English has become *The Tower*, no doubt the influence from Arthur Edward Waite.

PHYSICAL. An affair abruptly stopped. A theatrical coup, unexpected shock, warning to beware in business. The flame that removes the rampart from the tower can be interpreted as a release from prison. From the point of view of health; an indication that the limits of one's vital forces are being exceeded and that there is a risk of serious illness. If it follows an illness, a recovery after a distressing state.

INVERTED. Great cataclysm, complete confusion.

*

In sum, in its elementary sense, THE TOWER represents the transitory and fruitful constructions of man, always destroyed and always renewed, painful because they ruin ambition, beneficial, because they increase ever the wealth of wisdom.

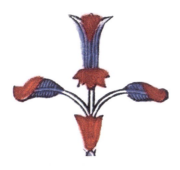

THE STAR
(L'Étoile)

PRINCIPLE

The number 17 = 10 + 7. 10 represents the universal cycle, and 7 the septenary, meaning, an extended radiation expressed by the universal spectrum and specified by the 7 sounds, the 7 colours etc. The number of stars on the card also evokes 7 = 3 + 3 + 1; that is, the two ternaries of the seal of Solomon, to which unity contributes a principle of activity. This whole is synthesized by the great central star, that symbolizes the emanation of divine power, that manages the involutionary and evolutionary force in matter.

GENERAL AND ABSTRACT MEANING

This card, supported by the psyche and the spiritual, represents; THE PRINCIPLES THAT PRESIDE OVER THE HARMONY OF THE WORLD. It imposes the beauty of divine construction to the imperfection of human construction, always in reconstruction.

It places, up high, in the stars, the active principle of cosmic construction, sources of light, and below in matter, a woman, the source of psychic life.

It follows the Tower to represent harmony, great universal forgiveness, the balmy that always comes after the fall, the appeasement of man before his rise.

FEATURES BY ANALOGY

The star represents the world on the physical plane. The great central star, grouped around it, seven secondary stars, synthesize the seven notes of the universal scale to make a singular harmony. This is evoked by its eight yellow rays, 8 constituting an octave, that is, a complete series. The 8 interspersed red rays, symbolize the same principle in matter, because in order for human need and understanding, it is necessary for the principles of divine intelligence be repeated in matter. The whole assemble forms the number 16, taken as 8 + 8, which, due to its repetition at the two poles, symbolizes the feature of perfect union between matter and the spiritual.

Under the stars, and on the ground, there are two bushes, whose green colour is the image of renovation. On one of them is perched a bird, a symbol of individual life, being able to bond to the ground or expand into space, and all the while to sing, to the morning break or to the joy of change.

The female figure is naked, thus showing, that the principle of harmony is not a clothed substance, and does not act more on one plane than on the other. The woman has only one knee on the ground, specifying that harmony does not rest on one point alone, but rather she must be ready, always, to take a step forward.

It is the great feminine principle that directs the current of the worlds and works for their evolution. She makes this current flow from two pitchers, representing

111

condensations, which allows for counting, sometimes with a spiritual influence, whose intensity is such that it cannot be effective, except if channelled. She manages this herself, to pour the dose that is befitting for man.

The horizontal pitcher held by the left arm, indicates a passive contribution, given to man at rest, as if by chance - as the one, who receives his fortune while sleeping -, while the vertical pitcher represents the active contribution, that is, the one that man receives through his work.

The woman is on the very edge of the embankment, because she is the source from which the water rises. This water is blue in colour, which means that this spiritual source is never dry, but it can only act by relying on the substrata of divine intelligence. This is determined by her knee, placed by her on the ground, whose yellow colour, chaotic and uneven appearance, leave her the option of sculpting it and shaping it in beauty.

She has two red pitchers in her hands, thus showing that it is through matter and from the currents of spirituality, that she must go to extract evolutionary harmony.

These two pitchers, represent the two poles of her fertility in matter. The pitcher of passivity is closer to her, representing the feminine principle of fertile action, a role more superior, than that of the masculine principle, being more susceptible than man, to be modelled for universal beauty. This pitcher touches the area around the genitalia, and its short waterfall, falling on sand, shows that it is physical receptivity, that communicates the instinctive vital currents of the individual, to matter (the ground) realized by divine intelligence. The active pitcher held in the right hand touches her knee, and the stream of the liquid it contains, flows onto the right foot. It is therefore a physical action, that produces an expansion in the emotional and sensitive plane, represented by the running of blue water.

In short, these pitchers and this water represents the great cosmic current, that never stops, always fertile and renewed.

ORIENTATION OF THE FIGURE

The position of the woman, three-quarters to the left, shows there is a reflective tendency, that goes towards its realization, a state of passivity that becomes active.

PARTICULAR AND CONCRETE MEANING

The name THE STAR has been given to it, as a representation of the illuminating and redeeming force, symbolized by the stars, which provide a clarity that comes from infinity.

UTILITARIAN MEANINGS IN THE THREE PLANES

MENTAL. A mental aid that provides a force to be used, but not directly, because you have to know how to use it. It is the inspiration of what to do.

ANIMISTIC. It provides currents of balance and liveliness.

PHYSICAL. Satisfaction, the love of humanity in all its beauty, the feeling of destiny, that animate men. Realizations of things, through order and harmony. In a matter concerning the arts, it gives idea of charm, that is, of radiance which attracts others.

INVERTED. Disharmony in destiny, physical harmony without duration.

113

*

In short, in its elemental sense, THE STAR represents the celestial light, that makes man glimpse a dawn of peace, hope and beauty, to sustain him in his work, bringing him comforts in his struggles and guiding him through his vicissitudes, and without ever coming short, in his participation of cosmic harmonies.

THE MOON
(La Lune)

PRINCIPLE

The tarot having been conceived, by reason of its evolutionary principles, according to the analogies derived from the number 10^{28}, the meaning of the 18th Arcanum must be deduced from the combination 10 + 8. Effectively, 10 implies the rest, that follows a completed cycle. 8, due to its indefinite description, represents an activity that is enclosed in itself, a double current that has neutralized, and these two numbers together express the paralysis, whose image is symbolized on this card by the darkness of the eclipse, in the mental plane, and on the animistic plane, by the rigidity of the towers and the encounter between the dogs, that oppose each other. Finally, on the physical plane, by the swamp.

---

[28] See General Comments on the Numbers 1 - 10.

115

GENERAL AND ABSTRACT MEANING

This card personifies THE INDIVISIBLE AND PERSISTENT LINK THAT JOINS THE PHYSICAL PLANE WITH THE ASTRAL PLANE; that is, with the plane of the invisible force, that rules the visible cosmos, and shows the distorted interpretations, that man introduces onto the coupled elements from these two planes. The two preceding cards indicated, one, the constructions of man, and two, the cosmic constructions of the Divine. Indeed, man has been endowed in his incarnation with very limited intelligence. He interprets the cosmic laws in his own way and distorts them. In this way, he is led to multiply, many times over, his own creations, to conceive them in the subtle planes, always wanting to give them a reality, that can only be illusory and that pull him further towards error.

FEATURES BY ANALOGY

In this card, the Moon, a symbol of man's imaginative creations, can only be a fleeting force, passing and not creative, not of divine origin, as evidenced by its human profile. The call of man to face his chimeras, and finding no point of support, but finding his own image like the reflection in a mirror. Yet it shows, by its rays, that surround it, that in its passing life, it still can exert an influence. That is why it also symbolizes the ebb and flow of human passions, as well as their reflections in the astral plane.

Its colour is blue, a creation purely of the psyche, built by the spirit of man, almost independently of his will. The rays in red and blue, indicate that this astral body can influence the material plane and the religious plane, but with little force, because the white rays, show that they are almost neutralized. The tears falling to the ground mean,

116

that what comes from the earth returns to the earth and that this creation of man in the astral plane, can fall back on to the earth and endow it with a moment of fertility. It is the ebb and flow of influence from the astral plane towards the terrestrial plane, and from the influence of the terrestrial towards the astral, both complete one another. These tears, droplets reversed, corroborate the scarce effectiveness of this body onto the earth, because what seems to fall like a fertilizing mana is, to the contrary, limited, and its red, yellow and blue colours, indicate, that man is not to expect to receive, necessarily, more support on the material plane, than on the spiritual plane or from the plane of intelligence.

The yellow towers are the symbol of force and the creative and transitory nature of a dream, which, manages to form a monument, that seems stable, but is nothing more than an illusion. They represent persistence in error, the refuge that one has created to trap oneself in the illusion of it.

The uneven ground shows that these towers seem, in the imaginations of man, to defy time, which he however from a base of honesty and solidity, cannot sustain.

The flesh-coloured dogs symbolize man´s primitive instincts, originating in the mental torments, that besiege him and that enter into conflict with one another. They bark to the heavens, venting out their chimeras. They open their mouths to feed on fluids, but this food only accentuates their error. Dogs, as instruments of the subconscious, also indicate the instinctive feeling of the errors of the conscious mind.

The crayfish, a voracious animal, with its claws, that pinch and embed, represents a state of purgatory, due to parasitic formations, that form in the state of the individual´s psyche, expressed by its blue colour, it is a purification of the lower psyche, that is experienced through suffering.

The lake represents a deep pool, and the edge that surrounds it, means that, no matter how deep the fall, man, if he wants to rise to the surface, can find the necessary support by grabbing on to the edge.

ORIENTATION OF THE FIGURE

The figure on the moon is in profile, seen from the left, which indicates a tendency towards imagination, inactivity, suspension, the halt of things.

PARTICULAR AND CONCRETE MEANING

This card is called THE MOON, that is, the chimera, because the moon, a light reflection of the sun, and not illuminated by itself, gives off an illusion, a mirage. It does not reflect reality, but rather manifests a borrowed life. It has no life of its own and makes the non-existent appear.

UTILITARIAN MEANINGS IN THE THREE PLANES

MENTAL. In the case of conversations, lies. In cases of personal work, errors. Mirages on all planes.

ANIMISTIC. Turbulent, passionate feelings, with no other outcome than disorder. Jealousy, hypochondria, chimerical ideas.

PHYSICAL. Total obfuscation. Clouded and an active state of consciousness. Scandal, defamation, secrets revealed. If the question refers to health; there is disorder in the lymphatic system, you have to change your environment, which may lack hygiene, and put yourself in a dry place, in the sun.

118

INVERTED. Instinct, the reasons for the mirage, the situation accentuates its effects, above the swamp. Confused state of consciousness however remaining latent, without action.

*

In short, in its elementary sense, THE MOON represents the chimeric dreams of man, conceived in the dark, under the influence of the agitations of his soul, under the obsessive push of swampy desires, but releasing him from his personal torments, once he is made aware of their pointlessness.

THE SUN
(Le Soleil)

PRINCIPLE

Along the same lines as the previous cards, the number 19 breaks down into 10 + 9. 10 represents the universal cycle and 9 the perfection, as if manifesting the product of 3 x 3, that is, the fusion of two ternaries one in the

individual, and the other in the universal. A fusion that represents a complete harmony.

19 can also be considered to be a result of 9 + 9 + 1. The two 9s forming a new ternary adjusting the individual to the universal, no less complete than the preceding one, and 1 that of unity. This other aspect of perfection represents a starting over, but on a richer foundation. Due to its evolution, this cycle, this world, needs a change in the planes.

The principle of the universal, by merging with that of the individual, makes matter vibrate. It lights up, takes autonomy, spreads its vibrations and radiates over its surroundings. This is why card XVIIII represents the concrete expression of this harmony with an image of the sun.

GENERAL AND ABSTRACT MEANING

This card THE TRIUMPH OF MAN OVER MATTER AND HIS EVOLUTION IN ACCORDANCE WITH THE DIVINE. It is opposed to the preceding card, that represented the action of man, separated, distant from that of the divine, while through its image of the sun, as its name indicates, shows the contribution of the divine, radiant and in beneficial form. It follows, that he grants the spirit a harmonious dominance over matter.

FEATURES BY ANALOGY

The sun is presented from the front, to show that its force is universal, and it does not have a side of light and another of shadow. It is represented with the face of man, thus indicating, that divine manifestation takes on the appearance of men.

The rays alternate; triangles express perfect alignment, emanating from this astral body, and these flaming rays, with their devouring effects, exerted, thoroughly penetrating man situated under their radiance and by the divine force they represent. They are of all colours, expressing the universality of their harmony.

The tears that fall from the sun, represented with the droplet pointed up, indicate a fruitful emanation, without loss, as in the Arcanum of the Moon, on the contrary, with a fullness, that is exalted in its downward approach. Their red, yellow and blue colours indicate, that they take their point of support on the material plane, on the spiritual plane and on the plane of intelligence.

121

The two beings situated under the sun represent a perfect union of the spiritual and the material. Their sex is covered to show that their quality applies to both to the active and passive sides of man. The one who rests his hand on the other's shoulder marks the active principle, while his partner, who puts one hand on the centre of the body and holds the other back, shows that he stores and reserves. This arrangement highlights the balance, that exists between them, because they are a creation of the divine plane. Their flesh colour indicates that the action of the divine plane takes place on the vital plane.

Their loin cloth highlights the demarcation between the high and the low, of the spiritual and the material, whose fusion has been indicated in the explanation of this card's number. They are blue to show that in this representation, there are no high or low principles, but only a spiritual emanation.

The small yellow wall, crowned with red, indicates the possibility of constructions in the physical, without obstruction, a possibility of realizing a harmonious, stable and solid construct.

The ground is yellow, to show that their base is constituted by divine intelligence.

ORIENTATION OF THE FIGURE

The pose of the sun's face indicates its direct, full, frank action and coming from above. The two beings turned towards each other denote a balanced and harmonious activity, because of passivity on the left, and of activity on the right, turning towards each other, impregnating one another. They are the counterpart, in positivity, the positive versions of the two beings from the card THE DEVIL.

PARTICULAR AND CONCRETE MEANING

The name THE SUN has been assigned to it, in the sense of radiance, because the sun that shines on the world provides vitality and harmony.

UTILITARIAN MEANINGS IN THE THREE PLANES

MENTAL. Elevated thoughts. Fairness in writing, harmonious permeation over the masses, permeation of thought over great distance.

ANIMISTIC. Chivalrous devotion, altruistic selflessness. This card only applies to good feelings.

PHYSICAL. Health and physical beauty. Elements of triumph and success in any situation that may arise.

INVERTED. Great adversity, unlucky, fumbling in the dark.

*

In summary, in its elementary sense, THE SUN represents the light always present in man, manifested in the activity of the day, veiled in meditations at night, which allows him to raise his material, emotional or spiritual constructions in clarity and harmony.

THE JUDGMENT
(Le Jugement)

PRINCIPLE

The number 20, that is 10 + 10, the number 10, a symbol of the universal cycle, repeating itself and because of this becomes polarized, expressing on one hand the individual and on the other the universal, but considered as 20, remains neutral, and expresses a state without activity, translating into stability. Man immobilized, looks at a cycle completed, one from 1 to 10, and the other, in the universal, from 10 to 20, and sets his goals to prepare for a new advance. He compares the knowledge gained with the debts owed, the conse-quences of his actions, and judges for himself in order to understand, whether the first phase of his evolution is over, which will lead him to the World, or if he will be forced to resume his career with the Fool.

124

GENERAL AND ABSTRACT MEANING

This card signifies THE INESCAPABLE CALL OF THE DIVINE AND THE SPIRITUAL PLAN IN THE MATERIAL WORLD, WHICH REQUIRES AN EXAMINATION, A REVIEW OF THE KNOWLEDGE AND THE EXPERIENCES GAINED.

FEATURES BY ANALOGY

In the symbolic interpretation of the figures and the details on this card, the angel represents the divine part, which man has left on the divine plane, when he incarnated into matter. The angel is represented by a human figure, because during man´s incarnation, he needs to see himself again and reflect on his true image. The two wings, flesh-coloured, show that what man has momentarily abandoned, he can now approach, and the angel's arms, red, indicate that this part of the divine, he can take with him into the material, although it may have been clouded over and been shipwrecked. The angel´s yellow hair indicates, that man is essentially a part of divine intelligence, but that this part he cannot bring with him into the material world. He is surrounded by blue clouds, because often man loses sight of the spiritual traits within, hidden to him, but these clouds can dissipate and he will see his own divinity rise again, with his spirituality and intelligence.

The trumpet indicates that man has always been able to hear the voice that calls him. It also symbolizes the vibrations that awaken his sleeping consciousness, to make him see the fruits of his actions and their inevitable consequences. The rays, by means of their yellow, and their red, denote that the divine intellectual part of man, even when not incarnated, mirror his incarnations, from to

125

which he cannot be indifferent by reason of the bond that ties them to him. The absence of blue comes from the fact, that the angel, being of the divine, does not need to display spirituality. The flag, white with a yellow cross, symbolizes the abstract nature of the divine plane, intangible to us (white), and which cannot be accessed without the spirit (the yellow) of sacrifice (the cross). This access is inevitable, because the divine plane is a devouring flame, that makes the incarnations of man move towards it, as the flag attached to the trumpet testifies, meaning, the emissions of the vibrations that awakens man and calls him towards the divine.

The two figures in front represent humanity, masculine and feminine, and their state of consciousness is symbolized by a third person, they are observing. He turns his back, thus pointing out that his state of consciousness is hidden. He is watching the angel, who is only known on the divine plane. He also represents the state of consciousness that allows man to find again, that which he left behind, when returning to source, and what will make it possible for him to incarnate again.

The demeanour of the two figures facing each other indicates, that to know your own state of consciousness, you have to abstract yourself and observe yourself in a mirror. The hair of all three, is blue, to specify that matter can only evolve when a ray of spirituality has touched it.

These three figures are not only representing man, but the awakening of most of the material plane, symbolized by the grave, in past acts carried out in the three planes; physical, animistic and mental. These forces also adapt to everything that lives on Earth, because when the state of consciousness is animated, everything that lives within it approaches their creator.

They are only three, and not a multitude of men, to indicate that consciousness only reveals itself to the life of an individual and not to us collectively.

126

The tomb is green, to indicate that the grave, the image of death, is not sterile, but is a great fertile force.

The ground is yellow and the figures do not emerge from it. Only slowly and with the help of divine intelligence will man emerge from the depths of his material state. The difficulties in this task are symbolized by the uneven state of the soil.

This card follows the Sun, to show that man has taken his origins in the vibrations of the force of the divine, but cannot harmoniously manifest them, if not through a successions of earthly returns. Although he remains in contact with the heavens through the divine part in him, there is a part of him that suffers, that belongs to incarnation, because if he is an integral part of God, he is also an integral part of the material cosmos.

ORIENTATION OF THE FIGURE

The position of the figures, the immobility, seen from behind, implies detention and inaction. Two of them turn a quarter, the woman on the right and the man on the left, they show the opposite orientation of activity vs passivity, which, on this card, leads them to detention, as they look at the figure seen from behind. The angel falls forward, his action is exerted by his trumpet, to animate the activity of the lower world towards the spiritual.

PARTICULAR AND CONCRETE MEANING

The name THE JUDGMENT has been given to this card, not in the sense of justice, but in the sense of comparison and evaluation of man by himself and on his own.

UTILITARIAN MEANINGS IN THE THREE PLANES

MENTAL. The call of man towards a higher state, his tendencies and his desires for elevation.

ANIMISTIC. No animistic radiance.

PHYSICAL. Good card, work of inventory, compilation, classification. Stability in a good or bad situation. Health and balance

INVERTED. Error made by oneself, and above all sufferings from an erroneous judgment.

*

In short, in its elementary sense, THE JUDGMENT represents man, awakened from his sleep in the material by his divine aspect, which forces him to examine his soul in all its nakedness, and to judge it.

THE WORLD
(Le Monde)

PRINCIPLE

Among the different combinations of the number 21 likely to agree with this card, the arrangement 20 + 1 and not 7 x 3 prevails, because the Tarot, when representing the evolution of man, must take its departure from the second series of ten, as it was done in the first. 3 x 7 = 21, which has been adopted by some Tarot interpreters, can only be accepted by subordinating oneself to a very secondary point of view, because this combination represents successive cycles of activity, that would be inclined to repeat themselves by ternary series and would no longer coincide with the Major Arcana of the Tarot, which have been extended to 22. 20 + 1 = 21 represents, by 20, a rich passivity with an activity 1, purposefully indicated by the central figure, whose raised leg indicates the activity of 1, and the androgyny; the agreement between the passivity of the 20 and this activity.

GENERAL AND ABSTRACT MEANING

This card means THE PSYCHIC AND SPIRITUAL ILLUMINATION IN A HARMONY MANIFESTED BY THE CLEARLY VISIBLE BALANCE IN THE ELEMENTAL ARRANGEMENTS OF THIS CARD. It symbolizes the perfection of man in the universal, his triumph over matter, his power over nature. It follows the Judgment, which gave man the means to reach the peak of his evolution, forcing him to listen to the call of the divine and to make a course alteration after each incarnation in matter. In a more general sense, it also symbolizes the perfect equilibrium of the worlds.

FEATURES BY ANALOGY

The central figure is androgynous. The two sexes united in one, without the ability to determine, which one of them dominates. In any event, this means, that the two poles are equivalent, always preserving their own superiority and the independence of their will. This figure sexuality is covered because, in reaching its apogee, man no longer reincarnates and therefore no longer procreates. This is indicated by the fine shawl thrown lightly over it and not by cloth, which would imply a desire to conceal.

Its left leg is bent to indicate, that it is active and not immovable. Its right foot, perched on a support that rests on the two poles of the wreath and not on the centre knot, shows, that it walks on a support based on it, and by the yellow coming from an intelligent manifestation. In its left hand, it holds a wand, that signals its power over nature. In its right hand, it holds only just with two fingers, an oval-shaped container representing a filter. It is the creative filter of illusion on all planes of nature, because man can have both the illusion of love and spirituality. The filter is in opposition to the wand, meaning that the illusion created

130

by man can give him a fleeting sense of royalty, but that everywhere, in the world of illusions and in the real world, as well as in the spiritual, man instead possesses a royalty, he conserves from his divine essence.

The wreath surrounding the figure represents the double radiation of the universal towards man and of man towards the universal. In the first, it means the currents of cosmic fluids, that maintain it, and in the second, the manifestation of the perfect aura realized by man on the three planes; red (evolved matter), yellow (divine intelligence), blue (spiritual mysticism). Blue is below to indicate that man, freed from the slavery of his flesh, is now completely in spirituality, and red, located between yellow and blue, in the centre, shows that matter regains his place between spirituality and divine intelligence. The red knots, above and below, welds these two poles together.

The four figures manifest the quaternary of superior forces, stabilized and balanced, in matter. This balance is the result of the four corner positions, which indicate that man has achieved full possession of his inner forces.

The eagle represents the wisdom of the heavens; meaning, the spiritual hovering over all creation. Its penetration into the depths of matter is symbolized by its red halo, and its action on all planes, which interpenetrate, through its body made of yellow feathers and feathered wings in blue[29]. The heavens, on which it takes its support, symbolized by the cloud, consists of the subtle and non-concrete elements, drawn in white, as with the spirituality created by man.

The being, above and to the left, depicts a human figure to evoke its ties with humanity. His red wings[30] mean man

---

[29] Translator: The card shown does not reflect Marteau´s text. The wings are green.

[30] Translator: The card shown does not reflect Marteau´s text. Wings are yellow.

131

cannot reach that state of supreme perfection, without having passed through matter and having been taken out of it again. His blue arms symbolize acts done exclusively in the domain of high spirituality. The front of the blue garment[31], white on one side and shaded on the other, represents the spiritual acts of man, some manifest, the other dark, obscured, unknown, can have great reach as well.

The bull, flesh-coloured, is the symbol of the generating power of the physical plane. It has no halo, because being essentially in matter, it is the brutal and undiscerning regenerator. Its wings mean that its symbolic potency extends to all life forms and to all worlds.

The lion, yellow in colour[32], is the symbol of the intelligent force, that presides over this universal fertilization, and that, as with the bull in flesh, is not the human material passions represented by the red colour of the other cards, but the worlds in matter, the concretization of divine thought. Its flesh-coloured halo shows that this intelligent force radiates onto the physical plane.

ORIENTATION OF THE FIGURE

All are facing ahead, with their head to the left, except the eagle who is in profile to the right, implying a strong direct activity, but with reflection, finding inspiration before the flight.

PARTICULAR AND CONCRETE MEANING

This card has the name THE WORLD, because being at the top of the Major Arcana, harmoniously makes concrete the efforts of evolution, indicated by the preceding cards.

---

[31] Translator: The card shown does not reflect Marteau´s text. Front is red.

[32] Translator: The card shown does not reflect Marteau´s text. Lion is flesh-coloured.

132

UTILITARIAN MEANINGS IN THE THREE PLANES

In a spread, this card means the feminine element, it cannot be interpreted or adapted to the masculine. It is a very individual card. If the querent is a man, it represents his thoughts, not his individuality. If it is a woman, it represents her personality rather than her thoughts.

MENTAL. Great power on this plane. Tendency towards perfection. Mental and control of the psyche.

ANIMISTIC. It conserves its power on this plane and means the elevation of spirit, feelings of altruistic love, meaning, neither egotistical nor sensual (an androgynous being represented on this card). Love of humanity. Tendency towards perfection. Inspiration in artists.

PHYSICAL. On this plane, to which it adapts with difficulty, it loses most of its power. Rich experiences. Solid and radiant affairs. Success and worldliness. Good health.

INVERTED.Ambush, inconvenience, failure. Renunciation of a triumph, of feelings. Sacrifice of love.

*

In short, in its elementary sense, THE WORLD represents man who is in balance with himself, finding support in the principles of the cosmos in wisdom and spirituality, the generative power and the power of direction. Man, who exercises his power over nature in line with the harmony of the universal laws.

THE FOOL
(Le Mat)

PRINCIPLE

This card is not specified by any number, because it would be necessary to give it the number 0 or 22. It cannot be 0, without the Fool then representing the universal indefinite, being mobile he is only but one step in evolution. Neither can he be described with 22; that is, by two passivities, as this implies an inaction, which is absolutely contrary to the appearance of the figure depicted on this card.[33]

GENERAL AND ABSTRACT MEANING

This card represents THE INESCAPABLE MARCH OF MAN TOWARDS EVOLUTION. Having not yet learned all the lessons of card XX and consequently, not yet reached the apogee of his evolution, man must thus walk his path through successive lives as a vagabond, indifferent of what tomorrow brings, his destiny hidden from him,

---

[33] However, in the adding up of the cards, this card should be regarded as number XXII.

because the advance constitutes the hope of an ever-better life, which requires of him to travel the long path of incarnation.

This card is normally placed at the end of the arcana, although strictly speaking it can follow any other multiples of 7; meaning after the Chariot (1 x 7) or Temperance (2 x 7), given its evolutionary qualities.

Although the Fool is found at the end of the deck, it does not indicate a confusing conclusion. It does not represent man, who has the book of all human possibilities, on everything that is guided towards him, of all the paths he must sever, of his burdens, and lead him to discouragement. On the contrary, it shows the return, at each birth with the amnesia of what he has been, and with the ignorance of what he will become. It is this languishment that allows him to open with a card that engenders a conclusion, not of his destiny but of the preceding 21 arcana. When man has reached his apogee, this card will disappear and the conclusion will be given in Arcanum XXI. The Fool also represents a link between the Major Arcana and the Minor Arcana, the latter describing man in his activities.

FEATURES BY ANALOGY

The stick that supports the bundle has two fixed rings, which prevent it from being withdrawn, indicating it is being imposed on man. It also means, that man is prevented in settling on any part of his path. This bundle is flesh-coloured to indicate, that man must always carry with him the inheritance of his fall onto the physical plane, because everything that comes into contact with physical life is a fall. Conversely it is his hope, a kind of Pandora's box that he cannot open but he can rely on, nonetheless. It contains his illusions and past experiences. The stick is white, meaning, neutral, to show that the bundle has not been created by himself.

The yellow cane, in his right hand, when in support of the ground, puts him in contact with the physical world and shows, that through his intelligence, he draws strength from the same roots that gave him birth on Earth.

The angle of flesh visible in the breeches of the figure, and on which the dog hassles, is the lowest part of man, the part representing the animal, that remains in him. It appears bare, because despite the habits, that he has created for himself in the course of evolution, he cannot get rid of it. The dog also signifies a remnant of the mistakes of the past, that persist in man in his march forward. This dog also symbolizes a lower plane of life, that tends to evolve and follow man. Likewise, it means that man has risen above the animal plane, not forgetting that, in his march towards his evolution, his fall has placed him among the ranks of lower creatures and that in his march, he must bring evolution amidst.

His yellow cap, with a red pompom, signifies the intelligence, that man must clothe himself with in order to travel his way through the material world. The red tip implies a material intelligence, not of the divine.

The blue ruff, the points of which end in bells, shows that the man in his footsteps is confused by the rumours of his past incarnations, and the noise it causes on earth, prevents him from finding his divine memories and forces him to walk. There are bells attached to both the belt and the ends of the blue ruff, to indicate that he is bewildered both on the material and spiritual plane.

The blue arm, coming out of the yellow sleeve, means that man, has the ability for intelligent thoughts (yellow cap) and can perform intelligent actions, but these will not be effective, if he does not know how to ground them with spirituality. Since man advances in the material world of his successive incarnations, he only does so through spirituality, as indicated by the blue tights and red shoes.

136

Though man walks like a vagabond through the walks of life, he is intelligence still, he is directed by divine intelligence indicated by the yellow of the soil and in order to show the difficulties of life, uneven ground. The tufts of grass signify active fertility, some are green, symbolizing fertilization on the physical plane, referring to the passage of the vagabond through incarnations. Others are white, symbolizing the fertilization, that he performs on the spiritual plane, during his disincarnations and consequently they are invisible in the physical plane.

ORIENTATION OF THE FIGURE

The Fool walks from left to right, but his head is turned three-quarters, implying the search for an activity, the reflection before acting and bringing about his evolution.

PARTICULAR AND CONCRETE MEANING

The name LE MAT (THE FOOL), which has been given to him, has the same meaning given to *mate* in Chess, (*échec et mat is French for Checkmate*), that is to say cornered. Indeed, he is overwhelmed by his burdens, which he cannot put down, pushed by the dog, stimulated by his bells, restless by the worries of the road, the obligation to move forward and the urgency of circumstances, that he will encounter on his path. He is also carefree in the sense that he is not aware of the obstacles of life and must deal with them as they come.

UTILITARIAN MEANINGS IN THE THREE PLANES

MENTAL. Indetermination due to the multiplicity of concerns that arise, and of which there is only partial awareness. Ideas in the process of transforming. Dubious advice.

ANIMISTIC. Turbulence in feelings, uncertainty in endeavours, vulgar feelings without duration.

PHYSICAL. Unawareness, lack of order, forgetting promises, insecurity, departure or displacement. Voluntary abandonment of material goods. Lack of visibility in affairs. From the point of view of health; lymphatism, swelling, abscess.

INVERTED. The Fool, a figure in movement, indicates that he has fallen or that he has been stopped in his path. Forced abandonment of material goods and fall without return or hope. Complications, entanglements, incoherence.

*

In short, in its elementary sense, THE FOOL represents man, advancing along his path of evolution, without concern and without rest, carrying the weight of his good and bad, he has acquired, stimulated by the ringing of his thoughts, the concerns of the moment or the lower instincts, until the moment in which the balance represented by Arcanum The World is realized.

THE MINOR ARCANA

GENERAL COMMENTS ON THE MINOR ARCANA

The Minor Arcana represent the secondary forces, that are subordinate to the principles expressed by the Major Arcana. They allow the implications, that lead to realities to be manifested, and are the steps between principle forces and their practical application. They make the Major Arcana concrete.

To put it briefly, the Minor Arcana give the details, that are derived from the principles expressed by the Major Arcana, however as one does not live in the energy of principle forces, it is necessary to express the implications of these in practical terms.

Like their seniors, they are subject to the laws of numbers. As they represent a material idea, they emit simpler expressions, therefore simpler images, and that is why their total number is higher than that of the others. They are 56 vs. 22, because as their quality is applied to the combinations in matter, they are necessarily grouped into series of four. 4 being the number representative of work in the material. These series have been given the following names: Swords, Cups, Coins and Clubs.

Moreover, as the Tarot represents the evolution of man, symbolized by the cycles of 10^{34}, and 10 implying all the periodic elements of the physical world, each element of the quaternary of the Minor Arcana, each with 10 repetitions, express all possible combinations of numbers in the physical world.

These combinations, being inconclusive by themselves, need to be defined through a new quaternary made conscious. 4 new figures result from this, which are

---

[34] See General Comments on the Numbers 1 -10.

naturally doubly polarized, namely; the Page and the Knight, the Queen and the King[35].

The basic quaternary visualized in this synthesis, with the objective to make concrete the Major Arcana, is extrapolated further into two groups of polarities.

The first, active and quantitative, represents an expansive energy and a condensing of energy, of which the Ancients have made the principles of fire and that of earth, and which, according to the symbolic images of the Minor Arcana, correspond to the Clubs and to the Coins, respectively.

The second, passive and qualitative, represents sensitive states, one expansive the other receptive, of which the Ancients have made the principle of Air and Water, and which correspond to the Swords and to the Cups, respectively.

This same quaternary, from an analytical point of view, makes this stand out as a form of condensation of forces; Fire, Air, Water and Earth, corresponding to the Minor Arcana; the Clubs, the Swords, the Cups and the Coins.[36]

This combination of the synthetic and analytical view of the quaternary provide the following general meanings:

The SWORDS represent the activity on the material plane, which in its most subtle and extended expression, opens an access to the spiritual riches of divine love.

---

[35] These figures, are given further introduction, following the chapters on the Minor Arcana from 1 to 10.

[36] The order and the relativity of card names would seem contradictory of data presented from certain interpreters of the Tarot. The reader will draw for him- or herself the conclusions through thorough examination, bearing in mind, that the Sword swirls in the Air, the Club is derived from wood, the generator of Fire, the Cup is the receptacle of Water and the Coin is the symbol of the metals the earth conceals.

The CUPS, a symbol of the receptive sensitivity of man, is filled with these spiritual riches and expresses them through a psyche that extends from the highest to the most elemental; from divine love to human affection.

The COINS concretize the riches by extending them to all the domains of the Earth, through the works of intelligence.

The CLUBS, symbol of material strength, use these riches to build, to cultivate and to consume.

The SWORDS represent activity on the material plane which, in its most subtle and most broad expression, creates access to the spiritual riches of divine love.

Regardless of their particular suits, each of these four aspects of the Minor Arcana are reflected in the other three; thus, the notion of universal love is found in all four, but is dominant in the Swords, as it represents sacrifice.

To more easily understand the sequential evolution, meaning, the tendency and the efforts towards a higher purpose of the four modalities represented by the Swords, the Cups, the Clubs and the Coins, it is useful to compare the previous card and the following card, not in the order of the numbers, but in the order of parities, that is, those corresponding to the same polarization.

The even or passive cards are lumped together, and the odd or active cards likewise, the former produces the internal work and verifies energy reserves, and the latter acting externally while making those reserves bear fruit by putting their activity into play.

REPRESENTATION OF THE NUMBERS ON THE MINOR ARCANA

The number of objects that appear on each Minor Arcana from 2 to 10, with the exception of the Coins, is indicated on the mid-horizontal axis, to the right and to the left, expressing the duality and thus indicating that these cards are passive -therefore impersonal and inoperative by themselves-, which implies a possible signal, a subordination to the majors, and which do nothing but contribute a property that the other cards direct.

Its role is overshadowed by the Major Arcana, and this significance is further accentuated by the Coins. These, in fact, do not carry any number – representing the circle with neither beginning nor end, and can therefore be adapted to all creations, just as money can be used for all of man's endeavours.

These four series of Minor Arcana, except for the Aces, are represented along two axes of symmetry, one vertical and the other horizontal. The first, characterizes the activity. The second, the passive significance, into two parts, separating the High from the Low - the Spiritual from the Material -, appearing frequently to make distinctions between elements of the card.

The Minor Arcana Courts, which, due to their human representation, indicate a personality, have names affirming this, consequently their predominance over the other Minor Arcana.

The Aces do not display a number, because they represent a synthesis of the series of cards to which they are applied, and consequently, they cannot take shape mid-air. However, by applying the number of the subsequent card, the unity onto another plane is transposed, this then reveals the original quality of the card.

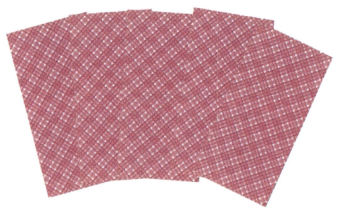

The backs of the Emrik & Binger deck

General Comments on the Numbers 1–10 And Modalities by which the Symbolism of The Numbers have been derived for their adaptation to the Minor Arcana[37]

1

The Ace represents unity, considered as an embarkation and as a synthesis summarizing the significance of the 9 consecutive cards of the same suit.

2

The number 2 is the symbol of passivity, polarity and the quality of gestation. Through passive polarity, it has no effect, but through gestation, it represents the substance in all growth.

3

The number 3, through 2 + 1, introduces an activity in the passivity of 2, which gives a direction to the gestation.

4

The number 4, a product of 2 x 2, contains a crystallization and, as the intermediary between 3 and 5, a transition. It represents therefore relative stability, and consequently,

---

[37] To the study of the Minor Arcana that follows, the reader must continually refer to the descriptions of the numbers.

things which are ordered and with a direction towards consolidation, towards security.

5

The number 5 is a number of transition, of passage, from one plane to another, because it is comprised of 4 + 1, with 4 being a complete number, to which unity is added, meaning, a beginning. The base of 4, on which it leans to generate the next number, gives it a sense of multiplicity and diffusion by radiance.

6

The number 6 represents a harmonious balance, being made up of 3 + 3; that is, two ternaries that are opposed to each other and of 2 x 3, implying the simultaneity of these two ternaries, and consequently, their equilibrium. In its elemental sense, it means a latent power, a potential, reserves from which one can extract.

7

The number 7 = 6 + 1, indicates, through unity, a force, and the action that uses the power contained in the 6. It puts it into play, maintaining its harmony, so that it meets a successful end. This is a number of synthetic performance.

8

The number 8 (= 4 + 4), joins the combination of the cross and the square; that is, the stability of the material plane with the inner life of the divine plane. It is a balance, that is not abstract, like that of 6, but that marks an end, because it does not need to be animated by other currents. It is the symbol of infinity, as formed by two linked circles, which, traveling in the same direction, develop one through the other indefinitely.

9

The number 9 represents the orientation of the abstract towards the concrete. The first 8 numbers indicated, matter was animated by the divine. Creating 9, which is 8 + 1, forces 8, which is perfect, to take one more unit; meaning, an entry into action, to describe a new cycle, implying a new penetration of force into the material, such as what takes place when a virtually conceived universe is manifested in the material, in order to create one´s evolutionary experiences.

10

While 1 synthesizes on its principles the other numbers from where things begin, 10 condenses them within itself, because it participates in each of them through its 0. This brings them together in potential and directs them to a new cycle, through 1 which accompanies the 0. It is, further-more, the number of reason and of calm, since, while with 9, the abstract is making contact with the concrete, by 10, it is now in equilibrium in the physical, since $10 = 2 \times 5$.

CONCLUSION

The Minor Arcana stop at the number 10, because if they surpass this number and reach 12, which is a result, they would no longer have a link with the physical and that would be inaccessible to human understanding.

SWORDS

ACE OF SWORDS

SYNTHETIC MEANING

The sword means power, the will. According to the analogic sense of unity, the Ace of Swords synthesizes the significance of the other nine sword cards of which it is the origin.

The mighty blue sword, held upright and with its tip lost

in the crown, signifies the spiritual, evolutionary start of man towards the High, thus expressing, what is best in him, and affirming it through a word or an action, whose manifestation is indicated by the red flower mounted on the tip of the sword.

The result of this state is revealed to man by the flowering enveloping the tip of the sword, that is, by the crown on the mental plane, and by the palm, a symbol of sacrifice, on the plane of the psyche, and by the oak leaf, a symbol of triumphant energy, on the physical plane.

ANALYTIC MEANING

The sword, which means projection, has been chosen to make a mental act concrete. Its shaped in a straight line implying the idea of a progression, that thought extends through the point of the swords towards infinity. The flash, thrown by the sword´s steel, when handled, symbolizes the inspiration of the moment, that makes one choose a path, aided by the point that attracts these spiritual currents.

It is a right hand which is holding the sword, the right signifying will and authority. The fist is turned to the left (opposite meaning to the hand holding the Ace of Clubs). The activity indicated by this sword is complex and must be shed with passivity, meaning, with matter, in order to prepare itself, since active intelligence manifests no power without an intermediary. The back of the hand is visible indicating, that the interior must remain hidden for the same reason; the manifestation of force, symbolized by the sword, can only be visible from the exterior, and its action should be indirect and held back by passivity.

The Ace of Swords, formed by two distinct planes, presents a spiritual significance in its upper part and a material significance in its lower part.

Held by one hand, this sword implies, that it is always up to man to seek a spiritual victory, and it cannot be obtained if not through incessant efforts. This sword has the shape of a blue triangle, which indicates that the search for victories must be clothed in spirituality and balanced by the ternary.

The arm goes through a circular, flesh-coloured, blue, flounce sleeve, indicating the action in a universe of physical vitality, crossed by waves of the psyche.

The red wrist, finishing in blue, specifies that the union of the two planes; the psyche and the material, the necessity to act.

150

The red grip, with the yellow guard and pommel, shows that the will of man, supported and protected by intelligence, is exercised in material activities.

The descending flames, of different colour, show the effective role of energy in the material world, and represent fertilizing germs, with which all things are impregnated. They also indicate that victories derived from energy are never from ego and that they are always poured out in beneficial rains. The variety of colours shows that their action extends to the three planes.

The rosettes of the crown, three red and two blue, specify that their dominion revolves around the spiritual and material planes, however with more power in the latter, because this is where the effort must be exerted.

On the band of the crown are nine ornaments. This ennead, too complex to be elaborated on here[38], represents the work of perfection, that man, in his radiation from the inspiration of the divine, is obliged to carry out in order to reach the quintessential matter, represented by the extreme points of the crown; the truncated rhombuses.

On the left side, the laurel branch, with its flesh-coloured stem, with its yellow and blue leaves and the blue flower from which it has been given birth, reinforces the meaning that victory can only have its origin in the spiritual

---

[38] Translator: Perhaps Marteau was thinking along these lines: On the band of the crown, there are 2 triangles, 2 diamonds or squares, 4 small circles and 1 double circle in the centre. Triangles represent creation and manifestation, Circles; cyclic movement, eternity, unity and the whole. Squares; the tangible, physical. Diamonds; purity, clarity and wisdom. Double circle, the third eye chakra, heightened awareness, clairvoyance, man's "self" within God. The circle, a point, one element, 4 points make a square, a square is comprised of 2 triangles, 2 triangles is polarity, that is, directional creation. 2 squares superimposed make an octagram, a symbol of rebirth and cyclical infinity. The Ennead, the 9 Egyptian Gods composing the Sun. The Sun is man enlightened or transcended. Thus the message of the band might be something like this; "Man an eternal being, a conscious creator, makes manifest the tangible by clarity of thought and with heightened awareness."

plane, and that it will only be achieved by force under its three aspects; mental, psyche and vital.

On the right side, the palm, flesh-coloured, yellow and blue, also birthed by a blue rosette, indicates an analogic effort, with the difference, that victory will come through an idea, without physical effort, but through sacrifice.

UTILITARIAN MEANINGS IN THE THREE PLANES

This Ace brings a conclusion, whatever the difficulties, it provides a consummation, because it is the synthesis of the other nine activities, and because the sword performs its task without flexibility and without diversion.

MENTAL. Intellectual clarification, precision and clarity. The Ace of Swords reinforces all intellectual power, because it comes from the mental will of man.

ANIMISTIC. Absence of sentimentality. This card puts its feeling in faith, mysticism or firm convictions.

PHYSICAL. Health. Affirmation of all progress. Ensures the good planning of things. Reduction of nervous tendencies.

INVERTED[39]: Mental laziness. Letting go. Lack of energy, weakness. In certain cases; violence. Abrupt halt in life. Homicide.

*

In short, in its elementary sense, the Ace of Swords represents the active force that man displays with firmness and understanding in achieving the triumph of his ideal.

---

[39] The innate quality of the Minor Arcana suit of Swords is not altered when the cards are inverted, but its effects are then directed, as a more or less general rule, in a pejorative sense.

TWO OF SWORDS

SYNTHETIC MEANING

In accordance with the meaning of the number 2, which represents a balanced stabilization involving a potential gestation, the Two of Swords manifests, consequently, by the black colour and the shape of the scimitar swords, as well as by their arrangement in quaternaries, the complete and subtle work of the subconscious, preparing the act of will, a primordial element of all mental activity. In other words, the three-coloured leafy rhombus, enclosed by the 2 swords, manifests, through gestation, its possibilities.

ANALYTIC MEANING

By itself, the 2 is comprised of two forces that, by reason of their composition are not manifesting themselves and would leave the 2 inert, but through the activity of the swords, which forces them to develop. [40]

As a result of this activity, each unit in the 2; one passive and the other active, is reflected in the other; meaning, what is active is loaded with passivity, and vice versa.

Concretely, it can be said that the passive sword resists and that the active sword penetrates, resulting in a quaternary.

The active vs passive external expression is indicated by the two interlocking semicircles in the Two of Swords. The duality of reflection, which is internal, is represented by the two swords themselves, whose points are enclosed in sheaths.

In general, this quaternary represents an equilibrium in play by the material elements; but the force that results from the swords, that is, from the primal forces, is a quaternary of principles, while the quaternary formed by the central flowering, represents the balance of the evolutionary forces seeded in the number 2.

This evolution clearly stands out as this quaternary doubles to form an octonary, a superior equilibrium. All this indicates, that the potential gestation of the number 2, will evolve through the activities of the swords, towards the other equilibria included in the first 10 numbers, which are 4 and 8.

In general, swords are represented as scimitars[41], to symbolize the characteristics and factors in mental activity, and not to emphasize their concrete actions. The currents, symbolized by the crossings, as they intersect, constitute an agitation in the spiritual and the material, in the self and in the not-self.

This form is also intended to indicate, that their number does not mean a count of swords, as if they were on

---

[40] In general, the even cards indicate internal work, and uneven cards external work.

[41] See in this regard an explanatory note in the Nine of Swords.

display. The two swords do not represent those of a duel, but rather the various impulses, the different origins, that constitute an act of will.

The black colour with, which they are drawn, is the tint of the invisible. The objective of which is to show, that the act of will, which precedes the mental act, carries in itself something of a secret, because it is triggered from itself. Its origin is not within our reach, we simply verify the manifestation of them, we remain ignorant of their profound source.

The swords take their start from the four corners of the card, to indicate the universal of the currents entering our mental activity, and their bases are wide, to show the power and mobility of the potential forces from which they emanate.

The scimitar shape is also intended to signify, that all the work that has just been described for the formation of mental activity occurs in the subconscious, where it may not yet have taken its precise shape, that it will take at the time of ultimate manifestation.

The wide black ends of the swords with guards indicate defence and containment, by means of material activities or intelligence, depending on whether their base is red or yellow.

The red and yellow guard bars are forces that constitute milestones and the need for restriction to be able to regulate the mixture of currents provided in the meeting of these swords. The internal work of the swords, the blue squares, above and below, indicates, that it is from the plane of the psyche. The yellow colour on the midsection corresponds to an inner, introspective and assimilative effort, and of a mental order.

The decoration between the swords, through its central white knot, from which a yellow and a red cross of flowers emanate, superimposed by another cross in blue, and by the double bloom of its leaves in four directions, as well as the forthcoming of its oval or rhombus-shape, represents

155

a synthesis of evolutionary forms, that mental activity will carry throughout its development in the following cards. The seven black stripes on each leaf indicate, that this activity must be aimed towards victorious achievements.

The four corner flowers represent the card´s link with the four planes or the four states, emerging like seeds ready to open. If you want to examine the process of their formation, it is pointed out, they are made up by a corolla of 5 blue petals and a red bud surrounded by a yellow chalice.

As the number 5 indicates, a transition, the 5 petals require a radiance on a different plane, then that of the Two of Swords. This transition gives rise to an awareness on the physical plane, protected by an intelligent activity, as indicated by the red colour of the bud.

UTILITARIAN MEANINGS IN THE THREE PLANES

MENTAL. Static equilibrium. Absence of activity.

ANIMISTIC. Wealth of potential feelings.

PHYSICAL.Contribution without impact, brake, hindrance. Plethoric health, slow circulation.

INVERTED. This card, being symmetrical, cannot be reversed.

*

In its elementary sense, the Two of Swords represents the stopping of a specific action, with a view to further enrich this action for a destined maturation.

THREE OF
SWORDS

SYNTHETIC MEANING

The 3 indicates, by deducing 3 = 2 + 1, the severance of two forces, neutralized by the intervention of a drive with a different nature. The Three of Swords confirms this significance by a penetration of the eclipse formed by the two scimitar swords, by a third sword, a large well defined sword, flesh-coloured, from which two branches of yellow laurel sprout, thus determining a will to overcome an inertia and to liberate locked forces, through an activity extracted from the vitality of the physical world, and whose decisions and effects generate mental knowledge.

ANALYTIC MEANING

The successive suit of swords will show an action, that is progressively moving towards fulfillment. Since it follows the Two of Swords, the Three of Swords is really already active, through its specific central sword, severing the two schematic swords and thereby creating a separation. This dissociation makes the polarity of the scimitar swords effective, which up to now, were no more than a potential.

The blade and the pommel of the central sword, flesh coloured, indicate its firmness in the physical, its red grip, the state it represents, which is still weak in matter. The yellow cross-guard accentuates this idea, by showing that this card must remain on a semi-physical plane. It makes a mental order stop between instinctive life, indicated by the colour red and physical life, represented by the colour of flesh.

The shape of the pommel as a closed lotus flower, as a ball, is the indication that the will to win must be based on wisdom, and that it will act in the physical.

The yellow laurel leaves crisscrossing over the central sword show, that the end will be successful, and they are supportive for the activity of the psyche. They embody the affirmation of their noble objective, symbolized by the white stems, a symbol of purity, and the glorification of the active principle.

The two swords in a semicircle have the same meaning as in the Two of Swords: Only the change in the yellow and red guard bars, above and below[42], differentiates their meaning. This is the case of all swords cards, depicting a central sword, however they do not alter the general meaning of the card.

Likewise, the same meaning applies with respect to the four outer flowers, but with more force, increasing with the number of the card.

---

[42] Three, Five, Seven, Nine because of the active power of the odd numbers, but Two, Four, Six due to the passivity of even numbers. The exceptions to this rule are: Eight, which is missing a sword, depicting instead a blue flower, since it represents a balance in the quaternary, and Ten, which has two central swords.

UTILITARIAN MEANINGS IN THE THREE PLANES

MENTAL. Decisions, doubts are settled.

ANIMISTIC. Liberation, enlightenment around feelings, clear perception of things

PHYSICAL. Sustainability, contribution of energy. Clear and direct progress in business. Very good health.

INVERTED. This card is interpreted with the point of the central sword directed downwards. Towards the top, it indicates a confirmation for any question, that involves a direction and ensures good outcome, because the point directed upward calls out and receives the currents from the above. Downwards, it implies a realization, it confirms that things will go well, because it is directed into activating matter. This card is never bad, except for a question of illness, because the point downwards, implies effort in separation of matter, indicating obstacles and resistance, resulting in delay in healing.

*

In its elementary sense, the Three of Swords represents a work of active consciousness deciding on specific actions.

159

FOUR OF
SWORDS

SYNTHETIC MEANING

By enclosing in its oval, a branch with all elements in full (stem, leaves, bud, flower, etc.), the four scimitar swords symbolize the constructive energy of 4, ordering and consolidating things to give them foundation in their future development. This is still closed in, albeit the branch that represents this is cut and ready to be used, when the oval is severed. In fact, the branch will have disappeared with the severance, that takes place in the Five of Swords.

ANALYTIC MEANING

The number 4 here, indicates the forces of the quaternary assembled. It is the work of the "self", represented by the cut branch, ready to be used, yet remaining in potentiality, so the following card, the Five of Swords, will be necessary in externalizing it. The central flower, with its blue corolla, its red bud, its yellow petals and its flesh stem, synthesizes the 4 elements and, by appearing in the state of a sprout, keeps its strength and shows, it is ready to be born.

The two blue and yellow leaves are branches, they form a communication and an expansion of the forces or fluids, and represent a realization. The yellow leaves below indicate the beginnings of activity, double in number and united at their base, to indicate the idea of a polarity in the germ of potential activity. The small black fruit, above them, indicates the evolving of matter, as well as a need for selection and elimination.

The red interior of the cut stem represents the life-giving current or blood, the force on the physical plane.

The meaning of the swords in a semicircle is the same as in the Two and Three of Swords. However, one will notice, as in the following sword cards, that the suit has its junctions above and below and laterally, with the blue and the yellow in blocks, this to indicate, that together these currents of activity is representing the swords making contact with the impersonal, and the kneading of these forces, while on different stages on their journey.

As this kneading is always blue at the top and at the bottom, and yellow on the left and right, it indicates that the mental activity develops in spiritual form on the higher planes and in the psyche in the lower planes, while it is dressed with a mentality of work of the inner self, while in contact with the external forces (the self is located on the left side of the card, and the non-self on the right side).

In this card the four outer flowers, smaller than in the previous cards, represent dispersions caused by the animistic activity of this construction.

UTILITARIAN MEANINGS IN THE THREE PLANES

MENTAL. Fluid richness.

ANIMISTIC. Safe and deep feelings, union without disturbance.

PHYSICAL. Creation, organization with great potential, that allows a realization, whatever the business. Very rewarding in spiritual matters.

INVERTED. If the flower is directed downwards, the card indicates unease, depression, sadness, a feeling that is clouded and persisting.

*

In its elementary sense, the Four of Swords represents joy, the inner ardour of man, created by effort and constructive activity.

FIVE OF SWORDS

SYNTHETIC MEANING

By representing four scimitar swords pierced by a large well defined sword, flesh-coloured, the Five of Swords symbolizes the breaking free of the enclosure in the state of matter of 4, through a strong mental activity, that draws its strength from the vital energies of man and gives access to a higher plane.

ANALYTIC MEANING

Just as in the previous card, the "self" was inside, the Five of Swords manifests this in the external. In fact, the branch has disappeared, only the four outer flowers remain (somewhat more open), indicating contributions, outwardly expressed as mitigation and hope.

The point of the sword, when penetrating the oval formed by the scimitar swords, having been enclosed inside, marks the

163

transition from the quaternary plane to the next plane. From a psychological point of view, it shows the phase in which man, by transposing his activity outwards, takes on a much clearer conception of the external. In other words, this card symbolizes an awareness, by man of his own individuality, as he relates to the universal.

The blade and the pommel of the central sword, flesh-colour, indicate, as in the Three of Swords, its activity and its firmness in the physical. The yellow hilt guard; an intelligence will preside over its action in the material, in directing it towards the spiritual, and the red grip; that its mental activity draws on reserves from matter already refined.

The shape of the pommel and the scimitar swords have the same meaning as in the Three of Swords, with respect to the guard bars and tops, the same as in the Two of Swords.

UTILITARIAN MEANINGS IN THE THREE PLANES

MENTAL. Willful and clear thinking. Decision. Comprehensive intelligence around events.

ANIMISTIC. This card is not very animistic, because it takes on an intellectual perspective of a question of the psyche. If in case of a union, this would be a marriage of reason and not of passion, because the activity, succeeding the Four of Swords, implies an effort in a passivity, that leads to a sacrifice of animism.

PHYSICAL. On the road to success. Move towards a positive outcome. Power of action over events.

INVERTED. Obstinacy, bungling, obstacle, because the point of sword enters the ground and is stuck there. Difficulty in business manoeuvres. Very serious stop.

164

*

In its elementary sense, the Five of Swords represents the decision, that man makes to settle difficulties, that are brought by his crystallization in the world of the elements.

SIX OF SWORDS

SYNTHETIC MEANING

To achieve the balance of two ternaries[43], one spiritual and the other material, as well as the activity resulting of this polarization, the Six of Swords is represented by six scimitar swords exclusively, symbolizing, consequently, increasing subtle currents of the subconscious. These have developed into a flowery branch, whose five petals, yellow, with a red flower, resting on a white base, meaning an effort to bring the mental into balance with the material, through an already evolved state of internal consciousness.

ANALYTIC MEANING

In a circle, the centre is considered a point of abstraction, since it is only known as the point of convergence of equal radii, while the circumference is

---

[43] See General Comments on the Numbers from 1 to 10; number 6.

166

visible and is in contact with the external, it follows then, that the elements destined for the interior of the circle will be all the subtler, the closer to the centre they are, and more concrete the closer to the periphery, they are.

This is why the black swords signify the currents of mental activity, in depth or on the surface of the subconscious, depending on whether they are internal or not.

What has just been exposed above applies essentially to the branch that occupies the centre. The comparison of this branch with the one in the centre of the Four of Swords shows the work, that has been done from one card to the other. This one is completed, it contains less off shoots, less elements, like the two yellow leaves on the Four of Swords, and the small black fruit, which represents a need for selection and elimination, is on this card closer to the chalice of the flower, which signifies a less coarse elimination.

However, the most important thing is the white support, under the petals. While the black colour characterizes the invisible; what is hidden, the white indicates what is not seen, because it does not stand out from the environment, or more generally, white light is the synthesis of colours and a symbol of animistic purity or of higher states. This white support therefore indicates the orientation of the flowery elements towards a higher state, through the support that is provided.

In the Four of Swords, the red bud (flowering of material activities) is separated from the seven yellow petals by a blue corolla, while in the Six of Swords the petals appear as numbering five and the corolla that separates them is red. The psyche (blue), considered necessary in the Four of Swords, allows for the necessary transition into the mental (yellow), and the bud disappears, since a white support (of higher order) is added to the developing work of the branch, and allows for a direct contact between the

167

mental (flowering of the yellow petals) and the push in the matter symbolized by the red bud.

The branches in these cards represent an internal psychological force conscious of itself. The bud indicates the effect of this force in manifesting itself in the physical, the psyche or the mental, depending on whether it is red, blue or yellow.

Same significance as Four of Swords regarding the red of the stem cut.

The four outer flowers are emanations from the branch that manifest externally.

The same meaning of the scimitar swords as in the Four of Swords, and with respect to the guards and the grip, the same as in the Two of Swords.

UTILITARIAN MEANINGS IN THE THREE PLANES

MENTAL. Creative ideas, concepts of affairs to be carried out, start-up, innovative ideas.

ANIMISTIC. Comforting effective protection. Utilitarian relationships between people.

PHYSICAL. Gestation, motherhood with hope of success. In the case of a business; balanced development. Harmony. Security.

INVERTED. Mental disorders. Tribulations in business. What is expected will be diminished or amputated. Inclination for evil or disharmony.

*

In its elemental sense, the six of Swords indicates the mental activity of man directed by him to carry out the ordering of and reconciling of material forces.

168

SEVEN OF SWORDS

SYNTHETIC MEANING

The blue sword, large and well defined, which in the Seven of Swords, penetrates the oval formed by the six scimitar swords, represents an animistic impetus, that releases the currents of mental activity buried in the subconscious. This card symbolizes, therefore, the enthusiasm that is put forward to verify the intimate knowledge, acquired through experience.

ANALYTIC MEANING

7 = 6 + 1; the 6 has accumulated riches through work, that balances the spiritual ternary with the material ternary. The force, which is added to the 6 here, is intended to bring this into play. Thus, the sword separates the oval and symbolizes the act of will that follows an emotional start and allows, through this internal shock, to make the work of the subconscious susceptible, to know the possibilities that are within. In other words, it is about man who having become aware of his equilibrium (through 6), is now

inclined to know himself through action, meaning, through the imposition of his footprint (the opening of the oval).

The centre sword is blue, because 7 is a number of sensitive action. The fight is carried out on the plane of the psyche with success, and the seven must embody the work of the preceding cards, spiritualizing their bungling through the blue colour of the sword. This sword has a single black line along its entire length, while the blade of the blue sword in the Ace has reinforcement from two additional lines at its base, and the flesh-coloured blades of the Three of Swords and the Five of Swords also have double black lines at their base, however as the Seven of Swords, is more active, finds less resistance, it is thus symbolized with just one single black line.

The yellow guard and the red grip are similar to those of Three and Five, but the shape of the yellow pommel is different, thus showing a more concrete activity and intelligence in matter.

The explanation of the scimitar swords does not change with respect to this card. The outer flowers likewise are similar to that of the Two and the Three of Swords, but with an increase of potency.

UTILITARIAN MEANINGS IN THE THREE PLANES

MENTAL. Understanding of things, clarity of ideas, balanced judgment.

ANIMISTIC. Harmony, psyche, altruism, union, agreement of opinions.

PHYSICAL. Harmonious start-up, achievements.

INVERTED. Depression, darkness, lack of inspiration, distraction in disengagement.

170

In its elementary sense, the Seven of Swords represents the test to which man is obliged to submit himself, in order to become aware of certain knowledge and without which his intimate sense cannot emerge.

EIGHT OF SWORDS

SYNTHETIC MEANING

The synthetic sense of the Eight of Swords is characterized by the blue flower inside the oval, which when placed in the centre represents the square consisting of two crosses superimposed, one spiritual and the other material. This symbolizes an internal balance between the two infinities, that coexist in the higher plane of man, thus indicating the possibility of his future liberation.

ANALYTIC MEANING

The number 8 is broken down to two squares (8 = 4 + 4), which like everything that is studied by analogy, differs a great deal. The square is geometrically deconstructed in two ways, by means of the two lines in a cross and by two diagonals. The former symbolizes the spiritual and the latter the material. Their union in the form of a square determines a perfect stability and being in the colour of blue, with the exclusion of yellow and red, shows that it is produced only through the psyche of man.

The four outer flowers, of which yellow is equally absent, are sensible manifestations of the inner and conscious work of man, who performs a fusion between the spiritual and the material. This fusion, when taking place in a harmonious balance, engenders in man a mystique, a desire for projection into the planes above.

Yellow does not appear, except when in the work of amassing mental activities in the subconscious currents of man. This is represented by the scimitar swords, work that is carried out outside of the will. The Eight of Swords takes on, exclusively, the shape of the odd numbered ones, in which the scimitar sword guards are arranged; yellow on the right, above, and red, on the left. As already explained in the Three of Swords, this is a representation of a quaternary balance and thus indicates that a divine intelligence, through this card, penetrates the activities of man.

UTILITARIAN MEANINGS IN THE THREE PLANES

MENTAL. Elevation of the spirit, understanding of spiritual efforts, mystical rapture.

ANIMISTIC. Selflessness, love that leads to serving the masses, preacher.

PHYSICAL. Stability in action. Better results from a spiritual order than that of a material order. Paralysis, due to the effects of the situation achieved, and which constitutes a consummated equilibrium, that would have to be broken in order to lead somewhere.

INVERTED. Since this card is symmetrical, it cannot be inverted. It represents an equilibrium from which nothing bad can come off.

*

In its elementary sense, the Eight of Swords represents the efforts to liberate man through an inner evolution, a consequence of his mental activities, and which is objectively translated into a reward, granted by destiny.

NINE OF SWORDS

SYNTHETIC MEANING

The central sword a large well defined sword with yellow colour, in the Nine of Swords, disjoins the oval formed by the eight scimitar swords, symbolizing a mental effort made to break the stability that the harmony of the 8 is inclined to create, thus making an evolution in ideas more complex and richer.

ANALYTIC MEANING

The evolutionary richness to which 9 can lead consists of; ending the system of individual units, because the last number 10, has in general, in an analogic sense, a closing of synthetic cycles in order to open to a perspective of indefinite periods.

The outer flowers[44] are the expansions, the needed work of mental activity represented in the Nine of Swords, in order to achieve clarity and understanding of its implications. In other words, these are the discriminations of man, that he is obliged to make in the course of his deductive search, from the information available to him.

The horizontal line in the middle of the central sword represents a slight break, due to the painful efforts of will, that man is forced to make to break the strong passivity of the 8.

The maximum number of scimitar swords stays at 8, the number 10 will similarly contain the same eight swords. This relates to the balance represented by the quaternaries of 8, which make a synthesis and allows for the currents of mental activity, in the subconscious, to be completed. A new activity, with the introduction of the number 5, would imply a transition, which would be incompatible with the purpose, that characterizes the number 9.

However, the idea of a continuity in these numbers reappears, not successfully though, that would be contradictory to what has just been said. Virtually, by the sectioning of the sword cards into four pieces, leads you to the number 16, which doubles and turns into 32 Arcs, if you add to this the sheaths of the swords in the four corners of the card. These four repetitions of 8 engender a dynamic equilibrium, that effectively sits on the 8 and evokes the notion of the indefinite repetitions of successive octave shapes.

To finish the point with what has been said on these sections, pertaining to the Two of Swords, it should be noted that the four points of division are located at the ends of the 2 axes. The meeting of the scimitar swords in blue, on the vertical axis indicates a psyche, that mixes the total number of swords at the top and at the bottom. The

---

[44] These have a smaller shape than those from previous swords cards.

number of swords characterizes, in this case, the number of emotionally based impulses, that enter into an act of will, while the interruption, in yellow, of the swords, indicate the act of will itself in its mental expression. Impulsivity is located on the vertical axis because of the active character of the latter, placing the will that triggers, and which is the fruit of the internal and external work of man, on the horizontal axis, by analogy.

The blade, the guard and the pommel are yellow to signal the intervention of intelligence, the grip being red and grooved in black like all the straight swords.

UTILITARIAN MEANINGS IN THE THREE PLANES

MENTAL. Activity, clarity, inspirations in everything that is of an intellectual order.

ANIMISTIC. Affected state; love illuminated by intelligence, powerful, not on the material side, but in its depth.

PHYSICAL. Brilliant affairs, conducted with mastery that brings success.

INVERTED. False judgment (the mirror of 8 is shadowed and reflects, deforms the cosmic qualities). Unjustified claims in judgement.

*

In its elementary sense, the Nine of Swords represents for man, the need to carry out persevering work to detach himself from the contingencies, likely to create in him a deceptive stability, which would paralyze his evolution, preventing him from penetrating the intellectual rays into the formation of matter and acquire dominion over them.

177

TEN OF SWORDS

The number 10 represents the final equilibrium of a first evolutionary cycle, and serves as a basis for the following cycles. The Ten of Swords makes this work manifest, at a time of improvement and transition, through the arrangement of two swords, well defined, whose sword points remain inside the oval of the eight scimitar swords and whose guards remain outside. This arrangement is the reverse of all the preceding odd number sword cards and symbolizes, in this way, the conscious direction imposed by man to his vital activities, both to ensure internal protection, through his knowledge of the balancing of forces, and to synthesize them into a unit, capable of being repeated again, with the benefits of its knowledge.

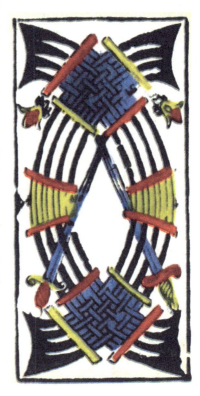

ANALYTIC MEANING

The image of the Ten of Swords shows, that it can be considered as represented by: $8 + 2 = 5 + 5 = 10$, depending on whether it is observed in its settings (8 scimitar swords + 2 defined swords) or successively, on the left (4 + 1) and on the right (4 + 1).

In the first case, 8 constitutes a state of passive equilibrium, put into fermentation by the internal activity of 2^{45}. In the second case, each 5, by their nature, implies a transitory state, but through evoking qualities and not quantities. The two 5's are of different qualities and in particular, opposite and complementary, because of the number 2, these two 5's correspond to a vibratory state, one on the physical plane and the other on the mental plane; translating the whole into passive work, meaning, internal work.

The points of the swords are inside the oval and are supported by the red and yellow guards of the scimitar swords, to show that they are not placed there to break the oval and act outside of them, but rather to discipline or contain, through protective arrest and a unifying will, the disorders that could result from the animistic kneading (blue, crossing of the swords) of the currents of the subconscious.

The situation surrounding the outsides of the sword grips indicates the free will of man, since by means of this disposition, he can freely take with his hand (analogically, by his act of will) the grips, to gather the scattered currents of the psyche (blue colour of the swords) and allow them to penetrate the 8.

The sword of truth on the right bears a black cross on its blade, and its yellow grip and red guard alternate their

---

[45] The reader is referred to the meaning of the number 2.

colours with the sword on the left. In addition, these two swords go through the four scimitar swords at their centre and come out through the central yellow, to end, with their points, in the yellow and red tops, thus showing the psychological and animistic activity ready to manifest.

The outer flowers count only two, and only on the top of the card, instead of the usual four, as in the cards from two to nine of swords, and this is the consequence of the perfection of the Ten of Swords and its balance: activity and passivity, and so only the flowers of the spirit have remained.

UTILITARIAN MEANINGS IN THE THREE PLANES

MENTAL. Fair, humane trial.

ANIMISTIC. Satisfaction and a mystical agreement on all feelings in a purified type love. Very high affection.

PHYSICAL.Philosophy before material things. Favourable attitude to events through self-control and emotional balance. Matters held provisionally. Health that requires a more emotional than physical support, chance of nervous Anaemia.

INVERTED. Sentimental disorder that distorts judgment.

*

In its elementary sense, the Ten of Swords represents the emotional sense of man, that when clarified by the harmonious balance of his experiences, allows him to act with knowledge of the facts, as well as to involve himself affectionately in the way a mother watches over and protects her creations.

CUPS

ACE OF CUPS

SYNTHETIC MEANING

The cup implies passivity upon passivity, because it is the inner work of man on himself. The Ace symbolizes, through the red part of the cup, a receptivity in the plane of material activities, based on the intelligence of the ternary, the pivot point of the world (yellow colour on the triangular pedestal) and the receptacle of divine thought made concrete under the aspect of the tangible inner shrine. This arrangement shows, that the cup is the point where the spiritual and the material come into contact. This communion, symbolized by the red semicircle, represents the host and the cup, closing in on its contents. This indicates that the internal work has been carried out in him, in order to balance in what he has been able to retain of riches from divine love with his accumulated knowledge in matter. This internal work allows man to become aware of himself, in the midst of imagination and sensitivity, man being the point of contact for the soul with the spiritual plane through mysticism, and through the taking, with elementary consciousness, of matter.

The cup, or what it contains, will always imply an internal elaboration, hidden in passivity and in the uncertainty of action.

ANALYTIC MEANING

The cup has been chosen as a symbol of essentially passive receptivity, because it is a container that, with its lid, becomes a sphere, meaning, a closed receptacle, which maintains internal forces and allows for their development in a closed cup.

The Ace of Cups opens the door from spirit to detachment and to the wealth of internal feelings and knowledge, accumulated by man in the different planes. Animism dressed in spiritual riches onto matter and into his various planes of sensibilities, where they live.

This card represents a notion of stops and suspensions, because what is in the cup is enclosed, symbolizing the elaboration, that man makes within, in the presence of the different aspects of things.

The Ace of Cups represents spiritual thought transposed into a concrete form. It is represented in the form of a cup to show, that man can envelop it and absorb it in his higher mind. It is crowned by a construction in the form of a shrine or a symbol of the holy Grail, meaning that the spiritual contribution of the divine is rich, which must be enveloped and protected, because any concrete divine thought that is dispersed, does not reach its objective and does not bear fruit. Its golden colour, as well as the pedestal, and the central red joining them, indicates a polarization between the high and the low; divine intelligence descends, through communion, to the plane of men and things, after having passed through matter, but since the shrine is more massive than the pedestal, there is a predominance of the spiritual.

183

The red cup supports the septenary indicated by the seven yellow turrets, which, with their seven red domes, show by means of 7, that the elevation of man must be established through all the vibrant scales of his soul, expressing himself on the highest physical plane.

The central motif on the top, in the shape of an ogive, crowned by three balls, and on top of a triangle, evokes the universal intelligence resting on the perfection of the triangle, a symbol of the trinity.

The three blue springs manifest the impulses of the psyche, that rush towards matter, while they signal their impetus upwards, first through the 3 red keyholes in the lower part of the shrine, and then through the red tops of the 7 turrets. Thus, this start requires a manifestation in the three worlds, and then an expansion into the universal, through the activity of the septenary.

The pedestal, due to its ternary shape, showing a triangle and four undulations on one of its sides, recalls the quaternary into the ternary, thus evoking in latent state the number 7, which is also found flourishing in the 7 elevations of the shrine.

The blue on the support indicates the spiritual support, which pre-exists in every communion, and which cannot happen without it. The 5 blue leaves, at the base, are a symbol of spiritual activity and affectivity (the 5 indicates a vibrating note in an activity.)

On the ground, which is partly flesh-coloured with black stripes, and partly white, specifies that this cup of animism rests both on the vital activities of the plane of the psyche and on the light from the abstract plane.

UTILITARIAN MEANINGS IN THE THREE PLANES

This card relates to the universal, because it is based on the septenary and essentially on the ternary. It is a powerful spiritual contribution and a great protection for the psyche. It does not descend down to the individual's mental plane, like that of maternal love, but is maintained in the higher planes. The cups are related to altruism and spiritual contributions and the Ace of Cups, by itself, opens the door to spiritual detachment.

MENTAL. Clear, inspired judgment, against which there is no recourse.

ANIMISTIC. Beauty of feelings, rising above personal detail. Altruism, charities. Education of the masses.

PHYSICAL. In contact with higher material things. Big enterprises. Ingenious artistic production.

INVERTED[46]. The protection is not withdrawn, but its effects are less felt and are not known to the recipients. Man becomes attached to the material and loses all spirituality. Gross materialism.

*

In its elementary sense, the Ace of Cups represents in man the intimate elaborations of the riches acquired on all levels of the mind.

---

[46] In general, reversed cup cards mean, readings concerning the physical plane are accomplished almost in remission. The cup upright means fullness; reversed, inability to receive.

TWO OF CUPS

SYNTHETIC MEANING

As the cups represent the essentially passive element of the quaternary of the Minor Arcana, it accentuates its passivity by associating itself with the number 2, of an equal passive nature. This is characterized as interior work, through a vital and flowery tree arising from a red base[47] between two cups and branching out in a triple stream, ending in two heads of animals with sucking mouths. This means the expansion of an animistic force, caused by the polarity of the cups, turning their origin into material desires and expanding into a triple current, that devours its own emanations. It symbolizes the intimate work of the human soul ordering and constructing its animistic contributions and absorbing them to feed its Chimeras, while preserving the knowledge of its mental experiences.

---

[47] Translator: In the Grimaud deck, the base is just one big red square, unlike the decorated Fleur-de-lis in yellow shown here. As a side note, the letters G M on this card, have yet to be deciphered.

ANALYTIC MEANING

The number 2 means balance through passivity. Duality, interposing itself between the two cups by means of a vital tree, implying genesis in all domains. The tree resting on the red indicates, that it takes its substance from material activities. The trunk of the tree, located between the two cups, shows that it is an emanation of them. This represents all the states of matter within the powers of man, animated by physical life. At the base, the trunk is blue, indicating that it begins with spirituality, to then open through the red collar, symbolizing material energies, that it needs to vitalize this tree. The white tree[48] which then continues, when combined with higher forces, synthesizes an extension, animistic in nature.

The devouring Chimeras are the spiritual reflections of the Two of Cups, meaning, a passivity of the spirit, in its internal fermentation. This is nourished by superior material manifestations, symbolized by the flower on top of the card, conserving itself, with a view to manifest in the future.

The importance of this card is great, due to the richness of the flowering.

The blue tree resting on a red base, a representation of the material world of instincts and lower desires, the inconsistencies of which is disclosed by the flat red, represents man wanting to make his dreams come true. It follows then, that the inconsistency of this base, preoccupied only by desires, that this card is about possessions and the manifestations of latent desires.

---

[48] The white, however, in the Minor Arcana, with the exception of the trees, does not imply, in principle, a synthesis, but more so a spiritual current, higher than the others, an illumination, an enrichment.

The red collar represents the development of these tendencies and of material organization, however while at the same time preserving a source of spirituality (blue in the centre), from where secretly (white trunk), the first intellectual outbursts emanate, this symbolized by the two yellow leaves, and then by extension in the form of the two Chimeras.

The central motif from which the Chimeras feed constitute a red vessel; that is, by support from activity in the material. This maintains a fluid, animistic part (blue) and a vibrational part (the petals of 5) that correspond to the fermentation indicated, and from which a red flower and intellectual flames (yellow) sprout. This symbolizes the mental experiences, the conclusions reached synthetically by this card.

The shape of the stem of the cups, in three visible sections, is the image of trinity, of which only one aspect is perceivable. The additional black lines (from Two of Cups to the Six, both inclusive) indicate the resistances in the material and as the black lines divide the cup into five sections, they represent the wholeness of man.

In general, the cups are yellow on the outside and let one perceive an interior of red. This indicates that the unfolding of passionate feelings (red) are carried out internally and are enveloped by intelligence (yellow) on the exterior aiming to cooperate. Blue does not appear on the cups, it appears only on the flowers or ornaments, since spirituality is generated by the fusion of intelligence with matter, a fusion that is an act of love.

UTILITARIAN MEANINGS IN THE THREE PLANES

MENTAL. Light after a time of darkness, due to the inertia provided by the strong passivity of the card.

ANIMISTIC. Intimate, solid force on which one can lean on, unless it is transformed into a devouring passion.

PHYSICAL. Matters rich in potential, which need an external moral or mental action to reveal themselves. Health: balanced, if you are well; stationary, if you are sick.

INVERTED. Disorder or destruction in the activity of emotional constructions.

*

In short, in its elementary sense, the Two of Cups represents an impetus of material desire, resolving itself in a wide expansion of the soul by feeding its instinctual and egoistic tendencies, leaving knowledge behind to be a source for future evolution.

THREE OF CUPS

The active and higher-order unit that enters the composition of 3 (3 = 2 + 1) is indicated by the upper cup, clearly separated from the two below by the branches of the plant, which has its roots between the two lower cups, but opens up around the upper cup with leafy flowery

branches. This symbolizes the evolution of the accumulated reserves in the two cups below into an action of superior animism. The evolution represented first of all, by the roots that have their origin in the instinctual state generated by the lower receptacles (the two cups below), and then through a passage of different stages to finally contribute purified elements, capable of making an expansion appear in the spiritual.

ANALYTIC MEANING

The cup above, a symbol of the higher consciousness of man, rests on a base strongly inspired by the psyche, as indicated by the encirclement in blue, from the red base and by the two blue ornaments that support it, directly.

This base has a central yellow (mental) motif from which white stems try to encircle the top cup. These stems are manifestations of the psyche, still too abstract and not synthesized by the forces above and without solid roots. It is about the thoughts the mind wants to plant in the physical. The blue and the red leaves indicate the pull towards matter, as well as spiritual realizations through physical energies. The twisting leaves[49] are in decline, they droop, representing the flawed forces of these thoughts. The two red embryos are such offshoots.

The two poppies, a symbol of sleep, that reach the cup in the middle, further underline the attractiveness of passivity and the flowering of emotional passivity under the effects of an action. They approach the centre of the foot of the cup and not its top, because there is a harmonious combination of the passive with the active, of no action, as 3 is a balanced number.

Finally, only the upper cup is encircled because, despite of everything, the form of thought is a richness that must be absorbed by the principal upper cup.

The two lower cups are situated on the plane of desire, they come from the preceding cards and are still devoid of activity.

---

[49] The black stripes indicate the obstacles to overcome.

UTILITARIAN MEANINGS IN THE THREE PLANES

MENTAL. As they are receptacles, the cups take on a spiritual value. The 3 is a spiritual insight for training in the material.

ANIMISTIC. Animistic realizations.

PHYSICAL. A spiritual contribution. Incarnation of the spirit in matter.

INVERTED. Exaggerated materialism. Superficiality. Excessive attachment to things.

*

In its elementary sense, the Three of Cups represents the sublimation of an instinctive receptivity in the riches of superior animism.

FOUR OF CUPS

SYNTHETIC MEANING

Due to the isolation of its cups and the rich flowering of its central stem, the Four of Cups represents the inner animistic work, that prepares for the elevation of the spiritual out from the material.

ANALYTIC MEANING

The cup represents a condenser of influences, here placed in the four corners of this card, that is, in the four directions of space. They symbolize the aspirations of cosmic forces in relative balance with the spiritual and the material. The ascension and inner work, with its manifestations on the different planes of the climb, are indicated by the centre stem with its successive blooms.

The bottom red limb indicates, that the stem takes its root in the depths of

matter. The predominance of material work over spiritual work, is already indicated by the number 4, which symbolizes the material elements, again indicated here by the leaves, that shadow the two cups below, thus forming a protection, a contribution of forces that do not exist for the ones above. These leaves are sharpened because of the activity from the psyche of the card. Contrary to the previous card, the blue of the leaves is smooth and without black lines, which means the ability to radiate onto all planes without encountering resistance; the exterior red confirms this activity.

The harmony of the stem, takes its root in matter, and is manifested by the flowering of the upper red flower, while the reduced blue corolla indicates a spirituality, but in a latent state. From this red flower emerges a white stem, ending in a blue flower with 5 petals on top. This stem signifies an escalation towards the spiritual through a feeling of expansion towards the universal, represented by the blue bellhop which tops it, translating the fullness of this feeling through the synthesis of the white.

UTILITARIAN MEANINGS IN THE THREE PLANES

MENTAL. The card is not mental, you have to trust your intuition and act without getting lost in analysis.

ANIMISTIC. Spiritual realizations, stable favourable contributions.

PHYSICAL. A well-established, well-started thing that will have stability and duration. Safety with regards to health.

INVERTED. Stagnation, obesity, circulation disorders.

*

In its elementary sense, the Four of Cups represents the reserves that man accumulates through his efforts of the psyche and that are translated for him into a benefit, a quality and as an extension.

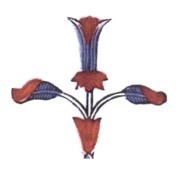

FIVE OF CUPS

SYNTHETIC MEANING

The Five of Cups indicate the deep intuition that takes charge of the animistic riches of the past and that begin to flourish strongly in the higher planes, preparing for the evolution of the Seven of Cups through the Six of Cups. This is represented by the central cup, crowning the doubly flowered root below, and from which a powerful bud emanates at the base of the flowering.

ANALYTIC MEANING

The unit that, together with the 4 (5 = 4 + 1), makes the transition from the material to the spiritual, is represented by the central cup. This constitutes the middle element that unites the work of the two cups below, with that of the two cups above and makes it all bear fruit. The work of the two lower cups is complete, as it has all its elements. The flowering representing this is; the roots, the polarized stems, the flowers and the offshoots. It is buried in the depths of man, meaning, in his subconscious, and this is why the central cup is encircled but without contact, as the subconscious does not have, by definition, any perceivable contact with us.

The two red flowers, in the shape of daisies, with wide petals, are the expansions of matter, that reach the foot of the central cup to help its evolution. Its origin in the four and its preparation towards the seven, is indicated by the four rounded petals, between which three other petals are inserted, which marks a birth due to its small size and a penetrating activity due to its pointed shape.

The work of the upper cups is represented by a strong stem, which expands into a blue corolla, an animistic support, from which two leaves sprout horizontally and which are rounded at the ends, this determines their passivity and indicate, that they are reserves of forces that constitute a spiritual support, black stretch marks are obstacles to overcome. These leaves are generated by an animistic impetus inspired by universal love, a synthetic feeling represented by the white of their stems, a synthesis of colours.

The flower above, in a protective blue helmet, shows that it has yet to undergo a gestation, that will allow it to reach seven through six.

The red corolla around the ovoid flower, indicates a reflection of matter arrested by the rise, because the evolution of the cups is not yet finished, there is a call for mastery. In addition, it must participate in this perfection.

Finally, the yellow ray, coming out of the blue helmet, indicates that the mental will finish.

UTILITARIAN MEANINGS IN THE THREE PLANES

MENTAL. Clarity in conception. Mastery over the elements in its presence.

ANIMISTIC. Mystical outbursts, maternal tenderness, sacrifice for love, impregnation of universal love.

PHYSICAL. In business; providing certainty to guide events or direct them with subtlety. From the point of view of health; delicate vitality, fragile health sustained by a great force of spirit and a nervous balance.

INVERTED. Detention in evolution, serious effects, sadness, discouragement, anguish, despair.

*

In its elementary sense, the Five of Cups represents, on the part of man, the organization of perceptions and sensitivities, extracted from the experiences of the subconscious, in order to gain momentum on a springboard of material feelings and to reach the spiritual plane.

SIX OF CUPS

SYNTHETIC MEANING

The six of Cups is made up of three cups on the left and three cups on the right, separated by a complex stem, comprising three parts; a root, a central flowering, a growth ending in a sprout. This represents, consequently the physical, animism and spiritual forces necessary to allow for, both involutional and evolutionary, work of man. Work also is implied by the number 6, as this symbolizes gestation, the elaboration produced by the interpenetration of both ternaries, one spiritual and involute, and the other material and evolutionary.

ANALYTIC MEANING

The stem essentially characterizes this card. Of the three parts that compose it, the centre, formed by the double cross, one red and the other blue, is a complex receptive element balanced on an arrangement of a double quaternary, a red physical, and the other blue of the psyche, circling around a bone formed by matter, represented by the small central circle[50].

This centre is supported below with animism made concrete, represented by a complicated root, meaning, on appetites and sensory impressions, more than on feelings. At the same time, it flourishes upwards in an element of superior animism, because this third plane presents itself, through its forms and colours, as an enrichment in a superior domain. It is a mystical, spiritual flowering, sustained by divine intelligence, manifested through the yellow stem.

In other words, the blue tip of the root is taken from the spiritual plane, so that it works as a support on the material plane, and the red tip above, means that the material plane takes support from the spiritual plane, to bring in a crowning on its own plane.

Applying what has been described in the "General Comments on the Minor Arcana", we can see when comparing the elements of the stem of the Four of Cups with those of the Six of Cups, how the evolution from the quaternary to the septenary is made. The blooms below on the Five of Cup indicated the role of the cup´s activity in quinary mode.

In the Six of Cups, the cups are purely symbolic and are entirely set apart to the right and to the left. They are more superficial than the centre axis, which is a subconscious flowering that man stores; the cups condense what his subconscious accentuates.

---

[50] Translator: Please note the Grimaud does not show this centre in white, only in red.

UTILITARIAN MEANINGS IN THE THREE PLANES

MENTAL. Active, solid, complete, final and favourable judgment, because the card represents a harmony between the spiritual and the material.

ANIMISTIC. The same meaning, but transferred to feelings; strong, protective and balanced feelings.

PHYSICAL. Stable business, guaranteed, almost unassailable. Robust health to abundance.

INVERTED. Discomfort, heaviness, but momentary, due to the involutional and evolutionary movements, that involves a constant kneading but leads to balance.

*

In its elementary sense, the Six of Cups represents the evolution of instinct, feelings and intuition, that man seeks to achieve in order to balance his perceptions.

SEVEN OF CUPS

SYNTHETIC MEANING

The Seven of Cups is characterized by the central cup, encircled by a branching covered with leaves, which has its root in the central cup below and culminates in two leaves that surround the central cup above. It thus symbolizes an awareness of the universal influence, that

is primarily in the lower world, and then develops in an animistic way, in fixing your gaze. In other words, it is a look at man, extending from top to bottom, allowing one to realize the complexity of individual consciousness and of universal consciousness, and to compare the two.

ANALYTIC MEANING

The unit that enters the composition of 7 (7 = 6 + 1), and that arises from the sum of two ternaries (6 = 3 + 3), is represented by the central cup. Every cup is a condensation of the psyche, and the central part of this card symbolizes the conscious centre of man. This central cup indicates a fold of consciousness after contact with the exterior in order for it to appreciate what surrounds it.

The leaves that encircle the cup, depicted vertically, represent potentials, and as they are not accompanied by any flower[51], they show that this card performs this operation with a strong activity, due to the particular force associated with the number 7 and, consequently with the unit that emanates from it $(7 = 6 + 1)$.

The two central cups, one below and one above, define the vertical axis of every card, and this axis represents the direct current from the spiritual to the material and vice versa. That is why, it has been said previously that the Seven of Cups implies man´s determination between individual consciousness and universal consciousness. The lateral extension of the branch, to the left and to the right, shows that this work is carried out both internally (left side) and externally (right side).

The four leaves on the card signify, with respect to those that are attached to the stems, possibilities of control over the thrusts symbolized by the white stems and, with respect to those above them, the limitation of conscious expansion and their penetration into the Above.

The top surface of the leaves is depicted in blue, a sign of activity of the psyche and of mystical feelings, contrary to the leaves on the other cup cards, they are depicted in red, thus denoting activity on the material plane.

In other words, the white stems, by means of the various shoots of leaves in different colours: blue - white -

---

[51] Let us remember that the leaf that, in nature, fixes energy reserves, represents a potential and is associated with the active and odd numbered cards, while the flower, a product of passivity, is linked to the passive and even numbered cards. See General Comments on the Minor Arcana.

red - blue and yet again blue, show their contact with matter, with which they are impregnated, which constitutes a basis for the penetration and the involvement of animism and the psyche.

7 is a powerful, radiant, luminous, beneficial number. For this reason, it has many white stems[52] representing a visible and superior push, that appreciates the power of the extension upwards.

The four cups, outside of the branches and located in the four corners of the card, indicate the states of consciousness suggested by the outside world, taken in their concrete or abstract aspects, depending on whether the cup below or the one above is contemplated. The subsequent cup cards: eight, nine and ten, are a continuation of this evolution of the psyche, indicated by the Minor Arcana, less dense, more spiritual, less fulfilling than the Seven of Cups.

UTILITARIAN MEANINGS IN THE THREE PLANES

MENTAL. Creative ideas. Education for some and revelations for others.

ANIMISTIC. Protective, invigorating and impersonal love; love for the country, desire for heroism.

PHYSICAL. Business conducted with clarity of judgment. Decisions without error. There is no point in weighing carefully the pros and cons, because the judgment arises intuitively and with certainty. Good health. Body in harmony, good circulation, athletic flexibility, agility.

---

[52] Refer to the Two of Cups.

INVERTED. Discomfort, everything concatenates. This card, reversed, can only be improved by the ten, which, as a perfect card, partially restores the broken balance.

*

In its essence, the Seven of Cups represents man's will to expand. The understanding and realization that is its consequence.

EIGHT OF CUPS

SYNTHETIC MEANING

By representing the 8 as shaped by 3 + 2 + 3, the Eight of Cups draws attention to the two cups in the centre, all the more so, since they are surrounded by a rich bloom, which thus determines the balance between the receptive imagination and the affective spiritual and material support. The cup on the left symbolizes the work of condensation of the internal feelings of man, and the one on the right the elaboration on feelings of expansion. The three cups above and the three cups below are the supports from the High and the Low.

ANALYTIC MEANING

The equilibrium of the two quaternaries, which constitute the essential message of the number 8, only appears here through the arrangement of the flowering. Its beginning, in

206

the centre of the card, on a double blue cross, with eight stems and eight flowers or leaves, show that this balance is manifested in the impulses and feelings of man, that come into play to coordinate receptive and creative elements of animism.

There is also a double quaternary arrangement of cups, separating the four cups located at the corners of the card from the four cups surrounded by flowering. The latter, being internal, represents man´s work by the psyche, as well as the balance in the games of his awareness. The four cups, in the corners, indicate external support. The cups in the interior correspond to the spiritual quaternary, and the cups in the exterior to the material quaternary. These together constitute the number 8. The first quaternary, due to its subtlety, is located in the centre of the card, and the second quaternary is transferred to the external; matter is generally represented by appearances, that is, by the outer dispositions.

The central blue flower, symbolizing the two quaternaries, emits an expansion towards the material towards comprehension and another towards the divine (symbolized by the yellow disk) in the form of a white line that upon accessing knowledge, gives it some substance. This represents what the balance of man ought to be.

The four flowers indicate the rich and passive character of the middle quaternary; the leaves, which are reserves of nature´s drives, activate the outer quaternary, extending high and low. The red colour on the twisting leaves denotes an activity on the material plane.

As with the previous card, the white stems have red shoots that show contact with matter, with which they are impregnated, and serve as a basis for their penetration into and involvement of the psyche, as determined by the blue flowers with a red centre.

The richness of the flowering indicates a great complexity, the coordination of which is done through the cups, each one condensing in itself the currents of the psyche, analogic to its position in the card.

UTILITARIAN MEANINGS IN THE THREE PLANES

MENTAL. Fixation in thoughts, obsessive ideas. To mentally detach.

ANIMISTIC. Affection between two people that do not detach themselves.

PHYSICAL. Stable business that is doing well, but needs to evolve. Bad state of health, that will persist if no intervention.

INVERTED. No change. This card is good or bad depending on the case in question and that of the surrounding environment.

*

In its elementary sense, the Eight of Cups represents a visionary proceeding with a balanced and safe judgment, that man, being passive however can only under an appropriate impulse detach himself from.

208

NINE OF CUPS

SYNTHETIC MEANING

Due to the ternary being presented thrice (3 x 3 = 9), the Nine of Cups symbolizes the innate balance of 3 in all its complexity and, as a consequence with the view from the psyche, inspiration from all forms of animism.

ANALYTIC MEANING

The three cups below are broken down to 2 + 1, due to the particular role attributed to the cup in the middle, revealed by the overload and the encirclement of said cup. This is depicted even more clearly, with respect to the central cup carrying additional flowering, thus representing the unit that is added to the 8 to form 9. These two cups, the one below and the one in the centre, are evidence to show the internal work, that is carried out in the 9 in order to break the vital stability of the 8. The bottom cup receives and regulates, while the one in the centre distributes. The blue agglomeration emanating from the lower cup is a concentration, from the central cup it is a diffusion. It follows, that the cup below performs a condensation of the spiritual force expanding to the right and to the left and seeks to take root in the physical world, through the blue and red leaves, with white stems, that are oriented downwards, while the centre cup, by benefiting from this work, spreads this spiritual force upwards, thus creating a harmonious bond, that must unite the physical world with the spiritual world. This diffusion only produces leaves, the reserves of actions, reinforced by their vertical positions[53], thus affirming the absence of any stagnation.

The implications, intermingling between the cups, show their common work, always taking a separate point of view that suits each of them and pins them down in their positions on the card.

Along these lines, the leaf symbolizes, in addition to activity, the respiration of man, meaning, his cosmic changes.

As the whole card is inclined to lead to the fusion of the two planes, there is a particular significance of the cups on the top.

UTILITARIAN MEANINGS IN THE THREE PLANES

MENTAL. Clarity of judgment, because the spirit is clothed with an intelligence made from knowledge.

ANIMISTIC. This card applies, from the point of view of sentiment, to collectives, altruistic work or those with a corporate spirit; to congregations, not to individuals.

---

[53] The horizontal position of the leaves induces passivity, as in the Five of Cups, for example.

PHYSICAL. Business in full progress, balanced from all points of view. Good health, cure of disease, resistance in taking action and endowed with great unsettled strength.

INVERTED. Disorder or confusion, because this card is decisive and brings as much confusion in bad as in good, maintaining continuous errors.

*

In its elementary sense, the Nine of Cups represents the harmonious animistic relationship of man with the world.

TEN OF CUPS

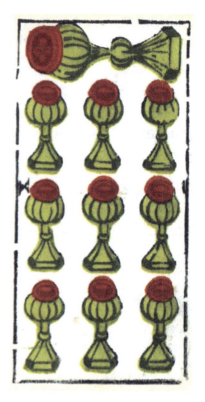

SYNTHETIC MEANING

When arranging the cups in series of three, halted by a large cup placed across, and the whole without any flowering, the ten of cups contemplates the number 10 in the shape of; 9 + 1, meaning, the arrest of the harmonious activity in 9 by a new unit. This stop is necessary to reduce the card to the passivity of 10; furthermore, the large cup, by its position, indicates that it spills into the others. The Ten of Cups thus symbolizes man, who is open, in the set of the nine planes, in receiving mode to all, so that he can receive universal assistance.

ANALYTIC MEANING

The number 10, which is represented by the unit placed next to the zero, signifies the end of a cycle, the halting of work, before the start of new cycle. This analogy is indicated in Ten of Cups by the cup on the top, blocking the way for the rise of the other cups. In the red opening of this transverse cup there is a depiction, that is both a flower and a mystical cross. This indicates a passivity in the activity, because this card, being the end of the series of the other nine, alternating between even and odd numbers, synthesizes them from the point of view of polarization, mixing passivity and activity into equal parts. The flower is no longer outside as a distraction, as was the case in the other cards. The red cross indicates a purification of matter through sacrifice.

The Ten of Swords and the Ten of Clubs approach 10 as composing of 8 + 2, while the Ten of Cups approaches it as formed by 9 + 1. The 8 + 2 arrangement represents an equilibrium (8), based on two poles that overlap, and encourage action, an impulse, that adapt to the energetic principles found in swords and clubs, while 9 + 1 corresponds to the maximum expansion of man (9), which does not allow him to act any longer and makes him wait for what the universe will bring in.

UTILITARIAN MEANINGS IN THE THREE PLANES

MENTAL. Achievements of the mind. Balanced judgment.

ANIMISTIC. Balanced, healthy love. Union that is complete in all planes.

PHYSICAL. Success in a company. Continuity in business. In case of a project, good results. Good health.

INVERTED. The harmony of the card means, that what is sought is not destroyed, but simply delayed.

*

In its elementary sense, the Ten of Cups represents the man who, having accomplished his work, turns to prayer and requests divine help to successfully follow a new path of his evolution.

213

CLUBS

ACE OF CLUBS

SYNTHETIC MEANING

The rough green colour, the branches cut off, held vertically by a firm hand, it is in the shape of a club indicating a material energy, constituted by a condensation of universal life, because the nonconstructive offshoots have been suppressed. The handling of the Ace of Clubs, is determined by the nine cards that follow, of which it is a synthesis, engendering a fertility in the three planes, symbolized by the cards raining flames in colour.

ANALYTIC MEANING

The club, a force con-densed, indicates a material energy, which is allowed to act on matter and give it shape. Contrary to the forward projection of the sword, this card is made to describe, when handling it, a circle, that constitutes a closed loop, that envelopes,

215

curbs and expresses its energy form in an elementary way.

The firm way in which the hand holds the club indicates the power found in the hands of man and his mastery over matter. It is the right hand, which implies, as with the Ace of Swords, will and command. However contrary to that card, this fist is turned to the right and the hand is presented from the inside, because the energy in matter manifests itself immediately, without prior moderation, as with the mental activity of the sword. The palm implies a direct action, the interior being visible and not masked by the thickness of the hand.

The Ace of Clubs accumulates forces and one becomes aware of the consolidations and the energetic powers that are in it, and through it. Man appreciates his strength of resisting the external impacts, by the means he resists, by his weight and by his solidity.

This is an active power of construction and realization in the material, which even has a spiritual component to it. This component is required by the arm that goes through a sleeve of flesh-colour and blue, circular, canonized, which indicates a material universe and its waves of the psyche. The red fist affirms the link between this card and matter and its essential material significance.

The falling flames in various colours have the same significance as in the Ace of Swords.

The club is represented as a wooden bludgeon and its branches have been cut because it is a spiritual zero, it cannot raise its branches upwards. It is strictly an earthly state on the material plane, and its green colour indicates its great force of fertility on that plane, and the red edge of the branch cut indicates, that the branches are made in the material world. The bottom end coloured in yellow means, that despite the purely physical and material state of this symbol, it takes its origins in divine intelligence.

216

UTILITARIAN MEANINGS IN THE THREE PLANES

MENTAL. Inspiration in the practical domain, an idea that arises in the current of the material, which activates it.

ANIMISTIC. Overflowing feelings, a bit exaggerated, more expressive than affective.

PHYSICAL. Active, bright affairs. Triumph by force. Superabundant health, a bit plethoric, which creates constant activity.

*

In short, in its elementary sense, the Ace of Clubs represents the material energy placed in the hands of man to allow him to resist external impacts, or to serve as a lever in helping him construct in the physical.

TWO OF CLUBS

SYNTHETIC MEANING

The Two of Clubs, by means of the two clubs converging towards the centre, which contains ornaments of leaves or flowers at an angle, this card expresses the balanced concentration of material energies, resolving themselves into elemental forces of potential, and if arranged harmoniously will hatch in the future.

ANALYTIC MEANING

As in the swords, the equilibrium included in the meaning of this card is conveyed in the arrangement of the figure as a quaternary; by the clubs, by the balance of principle, by the leaves and by the evolutionary equilibrium. But here the clubs meet in the centre and not laterally like

in the swords[54], which intersect at the top and bottom of the card. It is the inclinational essence of the clubs, to penetrate directly and internally, whereas the activities of the swords proceed by extension and envelopment.

Also, as with the swords, the quaternary of clubs comes from the superposition of the active with the passive, because the clubs have two faces; one active (the blow of the stick that is given), the other receptive (the blow of the stick that is received). In other words, the energy that is emitted and that which suffers. The four points of view are indicated on the card by the deconstruction of the two clubs into four yellow sticks and four black handles. The whole aims to maintain simple polarity, always balancing by means of the 4 energies.

The clubs represent the energy made available to man to overcome the resistances in matter, and the Ace having shown its principle, this card that follows highlights its application.

The two is made up of two clubs arranged as a St. Andrew's cross, framing the flowers vertically at the top and bottom and the leaves laterally. The symmetry is complete between the high and the low, between the right and the left, to show that the energy of the clubs can be exerted both in the spiritual and in the material, in the domain of intelligence or in that of the physical, for good and for bad.

The clubs are blue in the section of the crossing, thus showing that this concentration is supported in the psyche; meaning, that the energies of man must be, above all, gathered in the depths of himself, so that he can ensure his control and avoid the disorder, that would result from his dispersions.

The elongated black ends represent the handle of the clubs; that is, the part on which the force is exerted, and

---

[54] See the Two of Swords

its black colour is due to energy taking its origin in the invisible, that is in the current state of the subconscious.

The red bars are like that of the swords, forces that constitute stoppages and the need for constraints to contain and regularize the mixture of currents supplied to the encounter with the clubs. These bars are only red on the clubs, a sign of material energy, while on the swords they are both red and yellow.

The lateral leaves, as well as in those above and below, represent promises of achievements in the four planes. They are oriented vertically on the right and on the left, up and down, and denote psychological and assimilative, spiritual and material activity. The leaves are red, streaked with black, and leaf top in blue, affirming an activity of the psyche despite obstacles, and all emerge equally from the white stems, representing the synthetic currents and the hidden aspects of man's efforts.

Finally, these stems emerge from a closed yellow ornament, confirming the passivity of the number 2.

The white flowers in the centre at their base, five petals, with their stylized appearance, from where the equally white stems sprout, serve as supports for the leaves and the flowery expansion above and below. They indicate that these animistic riches take their base on a higher plane and operate in an internal and hidden way (white colour).

The 5 petals of the white flower, to which the 7 yellow petals of the sprout above correspond, indicate the transition from the vibratory activities of the message indicated by the number 5 to the message indicated by the number 7, a transition that takes place from a subtle plane to a plane of manifestation. The leaves imply an activity potential, that will be used for the evolution of these transitions.

The complexity of this flowering, compared to the Two of Swords, highlights the differences between the internal manifestations of these two cards: Both are very complex,

220

but the energy of the swords, as it occurs in the plane of mental activities, is of a higher order and is manifested through a quaternary equilibria, while the energy of clubs accentuates the transformation of energies, determining their vibratory form (5 and 7); one in an abstract and synthetic plane (white), and the other in a manifest plane (blue, yellow and red).

The richness of this manifestation in an active form of the clubs, also stands out for the lateral expansions of the quaternary of leaves, that take their origin in an intellectual base (yellow) developed trice (three aspects) and that emanate from a bone generated by the central animistic cross (blue).

UTILITARIAN MEANINGS IN THE THREE PLANES

MENTAL. Good judgment, justified by the value of the arguments, rational ideas, settled, practical but needs development.

ANIMISTIC. Trust, friendship, affection, kindness in simplicity.

PHYSICAL. Health on the way to improve. Business in preparation for future success.

INVERTED. The cards of clubs, in principle, with the exception of four and six, bare alter their meanings, as they are symmetrical. This cards meaning is not modified.

*

In its elementary sense, the Two of Clubs represents an inner potential that is inclined to expand.

THREE OF CLUBS

SYNTHETIC MEANING

The Three of Clubs are made up of two crossed sticks resting in their centre on a third vertical stick from which a simple four-leaf branch, symbolizing an inner discipline through forces that concentrate and coordinate the passive energies of the 2 in the centre of man, and whose job it is simply to accumulate the reserves of forces with a view to further manifestations.

ANALYTIC MEANING

In the preceding card, the four lateral leaves represented rich promises of fulfillment, consecrated in the blooming expansions of the high and the low. In the present card, the flowers have disappeared, and the central club has led them to their achievements. The four lateral leaves take on a different meaning; they are energy reserves. These leaves are similar to those of the Two of Clubs. The leaves make a twist, going from red to blue and they end in notch, which determines their activity both psychologically and physically.

This card has the same meaning with respect to the white stems as in the previous card. The yellow ornaments are still closed, the 3 barely frees itself from the passivity of the 2.

UTILITARIAN MEANINGS IN THE THREE PLANES

MENTAL. Insight into a matter; what is closed or incomprehensible is understood. Intuition of things hidden.

ANIMISTIC. Too expeditious to be emotional, demonstrating distance in affections. Nuances are avoided.

PHYSICAL. Very active business. A direction exercised with authority. Good, edgy, active health.

INVERTED. Not reversible. The three of clubs is great activity, always a comeback.

*

In its elementary sense, the Three of Clubs represents the putting into play of a necessary energy to become aware of man´s instinctual resistance, in order to discipline, coordinate and lean on them in subsequent work.

FOUR OF CLUBS

SYNTHETIC MEANING

The Four of Clubs, by the arrangement of its leaves and its flowers, reminds us of the Two of Clubs, however the handles in eight and its leaves in eight, evoke the number 8. The leaves and flowers are more expanded here, than in the Two of Clubs, and the 8, which only appears in this shape in a drawing, becomes virtual. It represents balanced inner work, that is supported by the previous even numbered card in order to evolve towards an even card, that combines both (2 x 4 = 8). In more concrete terms, it represents the evolution of passive matter through the utilization of material energies on all planes.

ANALYTIC MEANING

The balance of this card is derived not only from what results from the trait of the 4, but also from the orientation of the leaves on the top, the bottom, the right and the left, meaning, in all senses.

The two flowers, above and below, show the transition from 4 to 8, by the intermediate actions of 5 and 7. The even cards, meaning passive, cannot manifest their internal work except by the fruitful action of the odd cards, meaning active. This is also confirmed by the nature of 5 and 7, which are transitions and numbers of improvement.

The evolution of the Four of Clubs in relation to the Two of Clubs is indicated through the opening of the yellow calyxes on the lateral axis with its leaves, and by the transformation of the flower above into seven petals, which came from below, on the Two of Clubs, resting on a white bud. However, the card is still masked in the abstract, which is indicated by the two different looking flowers, born from blue and white stems, adorned with two small blue shoots, forming an ensemble of manifestations and completions.

At the top of the card, the 7 petaled flower, the most dilated, opens its crown, while the other flower, with 5 petals, closes up into a red chalice.

As in the Two of Clubs, the lateral leaves, as well as those in the top and in the bottom, represent energies put in reserve for the achievement in the four planes (they are oriented to the right, to the left, up and down); the psyche and the assimilative, the spiritual and the material.

The white stems represent synthetic currents (white light being a synthesis) and the hidden side of work. It will be noticed that from Four to Ten of Clubs, that the blue in the centre forms a grid with yellow above and below, signifying an activity of the psyche illuminated by intelligence[55].

---

[55] The sword cards from four to ten have red and yellow bars, in the center, and thereby, undergoing a different journey, these also finish in red and black. See explanation in the Four of Swords.

UTILITARIAN MEANINGS IN THE THREE PLANES

MENTAL. Decision, dominance in trials.

ANIMISTIC. Protection, certainty in affections. Spirit of brotherhood, since the number 4 is in the universal.

PHYSICAL. Good business results. Security in things at the point of the undertaking. Very good health.

INVERTED. Contributing to confusion. A score, an imperfect promise.

*

In its elementary sense, the Four of Clubs represents the fruitful work of man, reaching his ends through material energy.

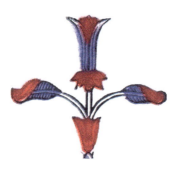

FIVE OF CLUBS

SYNTHETIC MEANING

The Five of Clubs indicates the work of transition through the central club and through the lateral flowers on the card, its symbol being 5. This club implies the energy put into play by man, who detaches himself from the material enterprise of the 4s, where the leaves constitute reserves of internal forces, that will realize a new evolution.

ANALYTIC MEANING

The Five of Clubs, regardless of the number of clubs, does not significantly differ from the Three of Clubs, other than in the large opening of the yellow calyxes, even bigger than that found in the Four of Clubs. From here the double lateral leaves emerge, and in the orientation towards the external by the spiral fold on each leaf. This means, therefore, a bit of reserve forces more expansive, than

227

in the other cards, taking the perspective of evolutionary realizations.

The arrangement of the axis on the card allows one to appreciate its psychological role; the central club, oriented from top to bottom, meaning, from the material plane to the spiritual, or vice versa, as the card is symmetrical. This follows the voluntary axis of man, indicating that it emits its personal influence in order to squeeze out the four diagonal energies. This is why the card implies a spirit of decision and freedom.

The leaves that develop on the horizontal axis symbolize, on the left; man's internal work on his "I", and on the right; his assimilation into the outside world. To facilitate this inner work, with the aspect of a new evolution, the leaves, which are reserves of strength, are located on this axis, perpetually pointing up and down to indicate the universality of this inner work.

UTILITARIAN MEANINGS IN THE THREE PLANES

MENTAL. Spirit of decision, that can lead to domination and authoritarianism.

ANIMISTIC. Dominating, protective feeling, a card of individualistic will.

PHYSICAL. Expected success, resting on solid foundation. Wide range business undertakings, transportation of goods: imports and exports (the central club being a bridge placed between two extremes and allowing their union by means of a circulation). Good health, with excess vital energy that is expended, sometimes leading to a loss of strength.

INVERTED. By joining the centre club, the high and the low without discontinuity and reciprocally. The card cannot be reversed.

*

In its elementary sense, the Five of Clubs represents man´s affirmations of free will, not to get stuck in the clumsy energies of the world of the elements and to rise to planes of finer vibrations.

SIX OF CLUBS

SYNTHETIC MEANING

The elongated lateral leaves, birthed by a moharra-shaped base and the flower above, with numerous yellow petals, depicted in the Six of Clubs, make manifest the riches generated by the harmonious balance of the two ternaries. One mental and the other material, which is included in the number 6 (3x2), as well as the activity of its polarization symbolized by duality. As a consequence, this card signifies the influence of the richness of the mental on material sensations. The mental understanding that disciplines the material desires.

ANALYTIC MEANING

As the leaves represent a reserve of forces, their significance indicates an accentuation of this potential, necessary for the subsequent card; the Seven

230

of Clubs, which, due to the extent of its action, requires a contribution in proportion. Furthermore, these elongated leaves show a form of elevation, an antenna projected into the four directions of the inner workings of man, indicated by these lateral leaves, while those on the branch above are a manifestation of outbursts in the psyche. The radiance is also manifested by the leaves´ base taking shape of a spearhead, whose objective is to create the activity, that is foundational in the work of growth.

In the Six of Clubs, the flower below has five petals, indicating that it represents the effects of the work done by the Five of Clubs and the support it brings to the Six of Clubs. It is situated below because, having fewer petals, it is less radiant.

The flower above, with its large number of yellow petals, indicates the richness of the mental relative to the material sensations, represented by the red on the flower.

UTILITARIAN MEANINGS IN THE THREE PLANES

MENTAL. Due to its wealth, it indicates inventions, favourable projects and actions that take shape.

ANIMISTIC. Deep love. Perpetuity; It is the Phoenix reborn. The Six of Clubs heralds this future, because it is leading to the seven of clubs, that of certain realizations, the Six of Clubs is on the verge of such realizations.

PHYSICAL. In business, slowness due to issues of duration. Continuous but slow development. From the point of view of health: Good, however at times lymphatic. Idleness that is suffered and not desired.

INVERTED. Accentuated slowness, that can displace pursuits, due to the failures of the things undertaken, however not entirely, something else appears.

*

In its elementary sense, the Six of Clubs represents the efforts of man to discipline his instincts and thus ensure the security of his future.

SEVEN OF CLUBS

SYNTHETIC MEANING

The Seven of Clubs takes on 7 as equating to 6 + 1, doing so with a white club piercing the Six of Clubs in its centre. It also equates to 2 + 5 by considering the two red leaves and the five yellow branches at their base. The first solution indicates an activity of setting out, sustained by a spiritual support, and the second a manifestation of a penetrative force into the animistic material domain, taking its origin with a strong mental flavour: All this work is aimed at maintaining the balance achieved by the 6, a balance that human imperfection always makes unstable.

ANALYTIC MEANING

The white on the central club provides the essential message of the Seven of Clubs, because it represents a complexity coming from a different plane, which superimposes, like that of the colours, the white light; the effects of which, constitute a superior support, and is translated into consciousness by sentiments of personal inspirations.

The branches represent an activity, that occurs in the animistic, since it is carried out horizontally, a particularly intense activity, as indicated by the five yellow expansions in concert with the blackberry leaves, whose red colour emphasise the physical effects. The white stems, in other words, are a symbol of impersonality.

UTILITARIAN MEANINGS IN THE THREE PLANES

MENTAL. Determination. Decision-making power on all kinds of issues.

ANIMISTIC. Great radiance, effects are more in the expansions than in depth. Expansive feelings. This fits rhetoricians, preachers and trainers well.

PHYSICAL. Businesses with great activity, top performance, a lot of determination in movement. Adjustments to mechanical issues. Very good health, with overflow of activity.

INVERTED. It is not reversed; Given the symmetry of the card. It implies much speed and decision.

*

In its elementary sense, the Seven of Clubs represents the possibility of success for man, through effort and active and constant work.

EIGHT OF CLUBS

SYNTHETIC MEANING

The Eight of Clubs, by limiting its particularities to two identical white branches, one above and the other below, indicates an expansion of man upwards, with reflections downwards, as a consequence of the harmonious balance achieved between the two quaternaries included in the number 8 (8 = 4 + 4).

ANALYTIC MEANING

It can be seen, that the lateral branches that appeared on all the preceding cards, and which was accentuated, in a very active way in the Seven of Clubs, have disappeared. As the horizontal is passive and concrete[56] in nature (the horizon, in nature, is in fact visible), it represents the internal efforts of man to understand and assimilate the reactions of the external world. The disappearance of the lateral branches indicates a work, that has been balanced

---

[56] See the Five of Clubs

and reabsorbed to transform into an upward impulse, with a downward return, in a harmonious similarity (the white stem), and since the lower branch being rigorously symmetrical, it appears as a reflection of the one above. This, by making the Eight of Clubs perfectly symmetrical, affirms the equilibrium of the 8, showing that inversion does not exist, and that everything indicated by this card will always be stable, whatever the circumstance.

These white flower stems, visibly sectioned, bear two small blue leaves on the right and left, where the leaves above carry a black stripe, and culminate into a flower, that has five yellow petals also striped in black, and a red bud with a black spiral, indicating as a whole, a mystical activity that meets resistance, a great intelligence in action and a desire for impersonality, albeit frequently hindered. However, the great passivity of the Eight of Clubs, compels it for continuous efforts, owing not only to the two quaternaries and to the work in a closed circuit of the 8, but also to the essentially material nature of the clubs, impregnating it with a certain clumsiness and a marked resistance.

UTILITARIAN MEANINGS IN THE THREE PLANES

MENTAL. Dullness, great passivity to overcome.

ANIMISTIC. Bungling in the approach to disputes, apathy that must be shaken off, as well as emotional slowness.

PHYSICAL. Businesses, with disorder, that must be reorganized through efforts. The business is better suited with food items and generally designate an abundance of stocks. From the point of view of health; lymphatic, glandular disorders, that a strict diet will bring back into harmony.

236

INVERTED. The solid representation of this card does not allow it to be inverted.

*

In its elementary sense, the Eight of Clubs represents the good conditions, the result of a general equilibrium, that promises man success, if he knows how to overcome the resistance of a stable state, to put his energies back into play.

NINE OF CLUBS

SYNTHETIC MEANING

The Nine of Clubs, stripped of all flowering and decorations has only one characteristic; the white guard placed on the central club, at the entrance into the bundle of the Eight of Clubs. It symbolizes a sum of experiences, that allow the activity of a master, an intellectual manifestation stripped of all fluctuations, of all parasitic actions, and always resolved.

ANALYTIC MEANING

The white bar of the central club, which by its colour represents a superior support and of universal order, differs from the vertical bars, which are found in the preceding odd cards. The Seven of Clubs, represented a harmonious aspect of active currents, indicated by the white central club, while in the nine, it forms the bar of the club and consequently represents a support and a reserve of forces of a higher order, which can, not only dominate the deviations of the central influence or make them deficient, but also coat it with an action of higher purpose.

UTILITARIAN MEANINGS IN THE THREE PLANES

MENTAL. Clarity of judgment, inspiration in the use of energy.

ANIMISTIC. Feelings of humanitarian, chivalrous nature, of sacrifice, of physical protection.

PHYSICAL. Inventions, business creations, to what is at the origin of things, creators, innovators. Radiant and harmonious health.

INVERTED. Being symmetrical, it is not inverted.

*

In its elementary sense, the Nine of Clubs represents the man who, takes advantage of the balance, that he has achieved in himself in the management of terrestrial energies, he knows how to determine the right moment of every action, by reflex or by intelligence, depending on what is involved. An immediate decision in time.

TEN OF CLUBS

SYNTHETIC MEANING

The Ten of Clubs shows two clubs with a white colour in the centre. They penetrate the blue in the central conjunction together with eight other clubs, and these are supported on each side, by branches also in white. It thus indicates a personal active balanced will, that makes its way through difficulties and organizes its energies in such a way that they constitute, the work of a new cycle. There are here reserves of forces supported on a higher order and on a spiritual basis.

ANALYTIC MEANING

The way the number 10 is broken down in the Ten of Clubs, is analogous to what has been adopted for the Ten of Swords. Effectively the deconstruction of 10 into (4 + 1) + (4 + 1), or in 5 + 5, is found in the Ten of Clubs by means of one of the central clubs in a group of 4 to the left and to the right, and by the two leaves, that with three white points of support, make a total of 5 left and right. The interpretation is the same, the difference being this number is adapted to a more material point of view. Knowledge is no longer sought through mental activities, as in the swords, but in the direction of work, through physical energies.

The blue crossing of the Eight of Clubs, under the superior impulse of the two white clubs, engenders animistic spiritual work, that is externally manifested by a luminous, balanced base (the white support of three subdivisions), from where they emanate, in the shape of leaves, expansions of energy and reserves. These leaves constitute, at the same time, through their points, fluidic respirations, that regularize the passivity of the 10.

UTILITARIAN MEANINGS IN THE THREE PLANES

MENTAL. Inspiration in the domain of the psyche.

ANIMISTIC. Elevated feelings for family. Foundation of a lineage, since the card represents a strong base formed by a matter illuminated.

PHYSICAL. Prosperity in trade or business. Balanced health.

INVERTED. This card cannot be reversed, due to its symmetry.

*

In its elementary sense, the Ten of Clubs represents the energetic and enlightened will of man, who with tenacity and independence is capable of manifesting the experiences he wants, resulting from the progressive management of his material energies.

COINS

ACE OF COINS

SYNTHETIC MEANING

The coin symbolizes the offering. The thing given as surplus, the gold of Saint Peter. Together with the other cards, it represents a supplementary divine contribution. This coin also implies the works of man, but with a perspective of external activity, and so indicates an activity in passivity.

SYNTHETIC MEANING

By depicting in the centre of the card a circle divided into three concentric zones, the Ace of Coins symbolizes an undulatory emission of the mental, constrained by the resistance of the environment.

This coin is represented in a different way, then those that appear in the subsequent cards. A simple black line limits its contour, because in unity it symbolizes the radiance, that penetrates everything.

The repetition of the elements drawn in the zones, correspond to the number of building blocks in the cosmos, implying that this project is in equilibrium. This is why it makes a sprout, through its contact with the environment, flowery stems with identical dispositions, above and below, demonstrating that they can manifest both in the spiritual as well in the material.

If the Ace of Cups represents the receptive side of man, followed by an internal elaboration, the Ace of Coins corresponds to the realizations of his interior manifestations. The first collects elements of the psyche into its cup, the second conceives of constructions, which remain in a latent state and whose gestations and solutions are indicated in the nine cards that follow.

ANALYTIC MEANING

The Coin has been chosen to characterize, not the internal kneading of the sensations stored by man, as it takes place in the Cup, but its disposition with a view to construct. In addition, due to its circular shape, which implies movement, and its monetary nature, which implies changes, it symbolizes the balance of the mental and the physical, with the perspective to make their union fruitful in a material sense. It becomes the necessary agent of union between the sword and the clubs, and between the cups and the clubs - that is, between mental activity and physical work - between the psyche and matter.

Man performs the work of a creator. He is inclined to project anything complex into his medium, in his image, and the flowering branches represent his concrete manifestations. He tries to project, through the diagonals, emanations of the psyche (blue) combining them with intelligent action (yellow) and vitalization (red), to end up, not in a straight line which would be lost in the abstract, but in a susceptible germ, withdrawing from itself a spiral, reaching its hatching, symbolized by the flower in bloom.

These branches also mean, that every power in the cosmos is kept in balance by the poles of spirituality represented by the branches culminating in flowers. The yellow of these indicates, that there can be no connection between spirituality (blue stems) and matter (red flowers) without divine and human intelligence. The flowers are tulips, whose 6 petals represent the 5 senses, plus one, the interior, an opening to receive, but also a closing again once it has received. It is a chalice, that receives and keeps.

The Ace of Coins represents the radiance of man in the image of the cosmos, and by its circle, it expresses his emanations, manifesting in regular waves, which characteristics are indicated by the depictions, that appear in each circle, namely; 16 triangles, large and small, symbols of the projections into space, and by the central flower of 4 rounded and 4 triangular petals, with 12 stamens evoking the fundamental numbers of any construction; the quaternary (the flower), the octonary (the 8 petals), the duodenary (the 12 stamens) and the successive extension of the octonary in the universe by means of 16 and 32 (the triangles in the 3rd zone).

In the centre of the circle there is a flower forming five other circles; the one in the centre, containing 12 points, evokes the notion of the duodenary, which in the cosmos is translated into the 12 planets or the 12 signs of the zodiac, depending on whether it is situated from the point of view of an active form or a receptive element. The 4 circles that surround it, contain the quaternary and its different meanings, the 4 elements, etc., and the 3 Trinitarian lines that each one includes, as well as the intermediate points that join them, show that these 4 planes are inextricably linked to the planets, their fate is decided together with the 4 elemental planes.

The triangles on the contour of the circle indicate a radiant activity in all domains and the area that separates these from the central flower, a conciliatory passivity between the principles and the exterior. The yellow colour of the coin shows, that intelligence permeates all activity.

The stems are the extension of this activity that passes through the material (red collar) and is transmitted by the flower, a symbol of harmonious fertility, after having produced manifestations of a psychological and intellectual kind, indicated by the blue in the stems and the yellow of the branches.

UTILITARIAN MEANINGS IN THE THREE PLANES

The Ace of Coins is the repository, the condenser of activities in all domains, in all parts of the cosmos.

MENTAL: Well balanced and fulfilling.

ANIMISTIC. Radiance, expansion.

PHYSICAL. A good luck card, to results delayed or advanced, according to its position with regards to the cards that surround it. Abundance of health. Extension of benefits. Affirmation of success.

INVERTED. The Ace of Coins barely modifies its meaning. Being symmetrical in general, it is tied to the beginning of the universe, where equilibrium is a constant, symbolized by the circle that has neither a high nor a low.

*

In short, in its elementary sense, the Ace of Coins represents man's desire to project onto the environment complex work, made in his image and capable of coming to light by itself for his benefit.

TWO OF COINS

SYNTHETIC MEANING

The potential for activity is indicated in all the coins, however it cannot be exteriorized in the Two of Coins, due to the inertia of the number 2. The number manifests itself as a general passivity, involving the neutralization of the active mental forces behind this card. Indeed, by representing a blue garland, enclosing the two coins and culminating in a flowering, the Two of Coins symbolizes an animistic or spiritual current enclosing the active consciousness of the mental and not allowing further future productions shine through, implying the number 2 is a gestation of potential.

ANALYTIC MEANING

The two coins, by means of the black shadowy lines encircling them, determine a beginning of dullness, since the Two of Coins represents the passive world, the material that opposes the spirit.

They have 10 undulations within and not 12, because the number 12 represents a completed cycle, which is not a good fit for the Two of Coins, which instead opens a series; while the Ace, being a synthesis, was associated with the number 12, the Two of Coins represents the setting in motion of the activities symbolized in a state of potential in the Ace of Coins. The blue garland is the spiritual element that animates it, because it links the coins, meaning the two poles, uniting them, it puts them into play, thus confirming the existence of the potential for action, to what was referred to in Synthetic Meaning. The red ends of the garland indicate its activity in matter.

The ∞, formed by the garland, which by its nature represents complete equilibrium, is indicated on this card but in a discontinuous sense, showing it cannot indicate some settings defined, but rather symbolizes an evolution. The Two of Coins, being the first card of the series, therefore implies progressive development.

The garland also indicates that the two units represented in the Two of Coins are not really independent, but are united by the internal current, that connects the two bodies. This appears manifestly in nature through the appearance of discontinuous mountain peaks, however all the while being linked to their bases.

These internal and universal currents can be explained by the fact, that everything that exists seems to be separate, even when they are necessarily linked. Indeed, no separation is possible, because all great currents of forces maintaining equilibria between these planes and without interpenetrating one another, emanate from the primordial unity.

The coins have been made manifest in this card to indicate the activity inherent in the coins even in their state of passivity[57], and as the universal current is never sterile,

---

[57] See the Ace of Coins

it follows, then the spontaneous fertilization of the two, flow in two planes; the spiritual, the coin above, and the material, the coin below, in a flowering symbolized by the leaves and flowers at the ends of the garland.

The red bud of the flower is encircled by a yellow chalice. The white stems represent a superior drive emitted by the feelings, which is manifested as a reserve of forces through the leaves and effectively, through the flower, which must come to light in matter. These sets of flowerings represent the complex developments on the different planes of the great current.

UTILITARIAN MEANINGS IN THE THREE PLANES

MENTAL. Support through an activity, going from the spiritual to the material, such as an inspiration implied by the great current of the garland, that provokes realizing of ideas or solutions to problems.

ANIMISTIC. Ease of approach by man on a spiritual or sentimental note.

PHYSICAL. Contribution of confidence, but in a subtle way. Support that takes its origin in the psyche, such as faith, and that facilitates a realization.

INVERTED. The symmetry of this card does not give it a sense of fix positions. It is not reversed, because it simply covers the principle indicated by the Ace of Coins with spirituality and matter, and maintains the balance that results from it.

*

In its elementary sense, the Two of Coins represents an intimate illumination that ferments the intelligence with a view to future achievements.

250

THREE OF COINS

SYNTHETIC MEANING

As with the Three of Cups, the unitary feature of the 3 (3 = 2 + 1) is indicated in the Three of Coins by the highlighting of the coin above. However, in the cups it was essentially passive, both in terms of receptivity and as it relates to the condensing element of coins. The abstract

yellow colour, and its circular shape, which allows it to roll, implies an involvement in mental activity, latent due to its passivity, but with an ability to orient in any direction. The Three of Coins, depicts a flowery stem, whose arrangement at the top is an extended reproduction of the one below, indicating a penetration into the universal, through an awakening of superior knowledge. An awakening caused by a resonance of the active forces contained in the two coins below, that have caused a spontaneous gestation in the higher planes, and also by the call from the coin above, all resulting in an impetus upwards, depicted as an expansion.

ANALYTIC MEANING

From the Three through to the Ten of Coins, the depictions of the coins differ from that of the Ace and that of the Two of Coins.

The Ace only has thin black lines, the Two already hampered by shadows, the coins of the subsequent cards are characterized by a thicker black border, that encircles the yellow centre.

Thus, they represent the potential of force imbedded in matter which, to manifest, requires an effort and a particular circumstance, an effort symbolized by the number that identifies the card.

The twelve undulations, that surround the centre correspond to the twelve forces of the universe, or put in different terms, the twelve great Gods of Teogonia.

In short, the black border of the coins illuminated by yellow ornaments, is a symbol of the universal laws.

Coins are very rich in spiritual power, which is imbedded in them. The coins and the cups are passivities, while the cup is just a passivity, the coins are a gift.

The Three of Coins is an influx of a spiritual order into matter.

The arrangement of the coins in a triangle represents a setting in motion for a given construct, and the point formed by said triangle constitutes the trajectory.

The stem is a stream, its white colour indicates a synthesized animistic manifestation of the forces above. Its flowers and shoots are blue and red, meaning, branches or fertility in matter or of the psyche. Green, above and below, a symbol of science and wisdom, but nothing in yellow, as this is transferred onto the coins to

252

show, that its depiction is surrounded by universal intelligence. The flower represents the psyche, where the intelligence of the coins is to be found.

UTILITARIAN MEANINGS IN THE THREE PLANES

MENTAL. Relationship with great insights and revelations of a scientific nature. The perks of the intelligence that accompanies love taken in its abstract sense, which is the highest.

ANIMISTIC. A contribution of confidence, proselytism, active mysticism, euphoric action on something decided.

PHYSICAL. Self-confidence in action relating to business, intuition of what to do. From the point of view of health; normal state, without excess vitality, skittishness. Instability.

INVERTED. Without cancelling what has just been mentioned, as the point of the triangle points down, it entails a general dullness, the effects continue to occur, but are less in tune.

*

In its elementary sense, the Three of Coins represents a mental expansion, that manifests itself through constructive and regenerative work.

FOUR OF COINS

SYNTHETIC MEANING

By placing in the centre of the Four of Coins a yellow rectangle with three stylized fleur-de-lis, framed by four strong buds ready to come to light, the Four of Coins represents not only a consolidation of material power and the balancing of the quaternary, but also an internal activity, which through its quadruple expansion, provides an enrichment and an internal sublimation, capable of taking up a sufficient force to expand into the ternary and reach the superior plane of the septenary.

ANALYTIC MEANING

The three schematic fleur-de-lis,[58] depicted as three emanations, are placed inside a rectangle to indicate that it contains in itself a ternary, which is superimposed by a square, thus making up $3 + 4 = 7$. Its arrangement on the card shows three stages of the quaternary in the Four of Coins; work through the four coins, of which the two below engender the support of a flower, two above likewise with their manifestations in spirit; a concentration towards a transition through the yellow rectangle, and finally an embryonic trajectory towards the ternary through the fleur-de-lis.

Coins, are inclined by nature to construct, to achieve, they reinforce the action of the quaternary. This is why the Four of Coins wants to show this affinity between the number 4 and the coins through those big sprouts and the additional rectangle.

Thus, the Four of Coins represents one of the strongest Arcanum among the coins.

Depicting the ternary, inside a square, the depiction, not of a triangle, but of a fleur-de-lis, is to signify the internal flowering, that takes place.

The square framing of the centre with the stems, leaves and flowers resembles the arrangement on the subsequent cards, albeit with the exception of the flower motif in the central rectangle, it is the central coin of the Five of Coins that forms this centre instead.

The white stems always have the same meaning of active riches, and the bulge on the white bone is the

---

[58] Translator: Please note, that the card shown corresponds to the description given by Marteau. In the current Grimaud deck, one will find a tulip on the Four of Coins instead. The Dusserre edition from Grimaud does however depict this card with the Fleur-de-lis in the centre.

representation of the concentration of forces generated by this card.

This is the only card of all the coin cards, where all the leaves turn from red to blue, implying very particularly on this card a fertility of the psyche.

UTILITARIAN MEANINGS IN THE THREE PLANES

MENTAL. Great intelligence in organizing and production, suitable for high achievements.

ANIMISTIC. Impersonal realizations; for example, the esteemed cleric turning towards impersonal love. In trivial matters, it is a higher current that goes beyond the pressing question and so is often unusable.

PHYSICAL. Very important business that has outreach worldwide. Good health, excellent vitality, longevity.

INVERTED. Generally, things stay the same, because of the universality of the ternary and the quaternary.

*

In its elementary sense, the Four of Coins represents the inner ideal of man, the conductor of his manifestations in all domains, giving him the power to achieve, whatever his support, in matter or in spirit.

FIVE OF COINS

SYNTHETIC MEANING

In its interior, a coin is encircled with symmetrically arranged leaves, and four coins furnish the corners of the card. The Five of Coins indicates a central edifying activity, which relies on the balance of the quaternary to send its reflections onto all the planes of matter, in order for things to be put in harmonious order.

ANALYTIC MEANING

The central coin symbolizes superior unity, which must act on the balance of matter represented by 4 (1 + 4 = 5), and which has attracted the rectangle with the fleur-de-lis of the Four of Coins, which now has become independent. The central coin has no contact with the leaves, except to those with moharra-shape, located on the longitudinal axis, which bring their points close enough to transmit their influence onto the coin or to receive from it, depending on the orientation of the card. This card is characterized by a central brain, whose purpose will be to build, since such is the inclination of coins.

The action of this brain can take place both in a spiritual domain and in a material domain, since the card is symmetrical, except for the minor alternations of the shades on the central leaves. However, the length of the leaves and the greater extent of red in this card than in the others, and the framing by the other four coins, indicate the predominance of activity on the material plane.

The transition to a higher plane characterizes the number 5. The chalice in the bottom only has four petals, while the one above, representing development, has five, these, in addition, are red and evoke the material plane. The development of the stems, their white colour, also indicates the active richness of the coins, active because the circle that surrounds the central coin is formed by leaves, which are force potentials. The lower part of the card is naturally enhanced by the bud with the four-petaled chalice, which stem is reinforced by a bulge, a white bone, representing the concentration of forces generated by the Four of Coins, where this bone already appeared.

UTILITARIAN MEANINGS IN THE THREE PLANES

MENTAL. Setting in motion (central coin) that rests on the spiritual (coins above) and on matter (coins below). Projects that clearly take shape.

ANIMISTIC. The forming of relationships, in friendships or to marriage. Strengthening of affections.

PHYSICAL. Business where performance is assured, growing customer base. Security in health.

INVERTED. Little change, small decrease in the flowering of what has appeared, in the results being prepared.

*

In its elementary sense, the Five of Coins represents man appealing to his active awareness in all domains, applying his building brain to harmonious and balanced activity.

SIX OF COINS

SYNTHETIC MEANING

By representing the inverted triangles (6 = 2 x 3), between which a wide cross, with leafy branches, up and down, is sandwiched, the Six of Coins symbolizes the work of involution and evolution, which man is obliged to do on himself, through alternating efforts directed upwards and downwards, preparing for an evolution in his internal and external structure, in his psyche and body, internal in him and external to him.

ANALYTIC MEANING

The cross represents the work of conscience, as it is in the centre and extends to all the coins. It takes its support on its pivot (central red circle) on the material plane represented by the small red cross of San Andres, indicating the principle. The extension of its blue colour and the complexity of its shape denotes the importance of the sensitive work of the subconscious in this card, and its red flowery branches, located on the horizontal axis, show the fruitful nature of man´s animistic expansions towards the material.

The leaves, always forces of potential, indicate attempts at exploration of the above and below. Blue on the inside and turning to red on the outside, implies fertility in matter; the white stem that supports them, is a synthesis of currents on different planes, whose work is manifested through outbursts of activity in the material, represented by the red buds at the bifurcation points of the white stems.

UTILITARIAN MEANINGS IN THE THREE PLANES

MENTAL. Efforts necessary for success (sacrifice is implied by this card). Knowing how to do what is unpleasant, aware when you have the obligation to do so.

ANIMISTIC. Renunciation of oneself, renunciation in the domain of affection.

PHYSICAL. Businesses whose success can only be obtained at the price of a partial sacrifice. From the point of view of health; nervous depressions, due to energy losses, due to the absorption in matter, repairable, however carries with it a momentary deficiency.

INVERTED. This card, being symmetrical, is not reversed, balance being its main meaning.

*

In its elementary sense, the Six of Coins represents the internal improvements, that man makes through an effort to reconcile the currents from above with those from below, in order to balance his alignments.

SEVEN OF COINS

SYNTHETIC MEANING

By arranging the coins in the form of a triangle in the section above and in the shape of a square in the section below, the Seven of Coins approaches the number 7 as formed by 3 + 4, respecting the fundamental unit, that characterizes the 7 in a significant way (6 + 1). The coin

forming the point of the triangle distinguishes itself by the encirclement of leaves. This arrangement symbolizes a harmonious expansion of man´s consciousness. The fruits of the reserves accumulated by man.

ANALYTIC MEANING

The square represents a stabilization produced by the play of the four elements, which constitutes the principle of material activity, forcing it to settle in the restricted domain of the physical world.

The point of the triangle, in shape of a coin, symbolizes the fertile energy of the 7. As it touches the quaternary, it frees itself from crystallization and its riches can be exploited, represented by the white stem, sandwiched between the four coins of the base, born from the red and blue motif and adorned with two horizontal leaves of alternating colours, one blue and the other red. The double expansion of this white stem, splitting off from the central stem, now blue and red, into two leaves of alternating colours, with two off shoots, one blue and the other red, finishing off with two other leaves of alternating colours, that meet at the top. This shows the exhilarating riches produced, taking place in beautiful detail, with the encircled coin placed on an elevated plane.

Another detail stands out, which indicates the happy balance of this card, when the two coins above and the two coins below are viewed sandwiched, with a triangle in the centre of the card with its point up. The triangle indicates balance by nature, and its total involvement denotes the extension of its means, its origin arising from the physical plane. The leaves, in addition to being forces of potential, symbolize impulses, seen by their activity.

UTILITARIAN MEANINGS IN THE THREE PLANES

MENTAL. Great activity of spirit with ease in exposure and organization. Accomplishment can be derived from brain power.

ANIMISTC. Animistic radiance, a vibrant feeling that goes beyond the framework of everyday life and reaches the public.

PHYSICAL. Large and active business. Good health, internal drive.

INVERTED. Clumsiness and heaviness, an unfavourable position in a matter from which it will be painful to escape. Arrest and bankruptcy.

*

In its elementary sense, the Seven of Coins represents man's incitement to action and the decisions he must make, in order to create a steady state for himself.

EIGHT OF COINS

SYNTHETIC MEANING

Through the regular arrangement of the coins, the symmetry of the card and the central cross, which impacts and infiltrates in all directions, the Eight of Coins represents the harmonious balance of the number 8. It symbolizes the internal perception of the universal influence, that penetrates everywhere. It differs in the various planes and allows for establishment of logical constructions both above and below.

ANALYTIC MEANING

Comparing this card to the Six of Coins, allows us to establish the evolution, that has taken place with the branches under the effects of the active forces in the Seven of Coins. The centre that corresponds to the inner work of consciousness, is covered with a construction very complex, comprising a

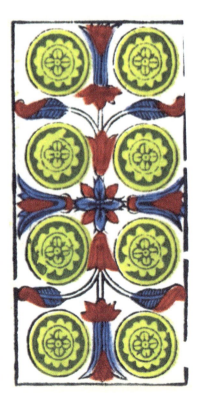

blue cross, therefore of the psyche, which dominates the red quaternary (diagonally) of the material, and with it adjusted, gives birth to the eight points of radii.

This grouping, which represents the fusion of the spiritual plane with the material plane and the radiance, that results from it, generates four similar flowers, located at the extremes of the two axes on the card, thus implying a particular preponderance; the upper flower is open to receive from the one below, however it is half closed, it´s in matter. The five red petals indicate that both are expanded in the physical, and through the number 5 they announce a possibility of vibrating or traveling onto a higher plane. The flowers, in the centre, are reflections of the other two, meaning, aware of their assimilation, through the inner and outer workings of man.

All the coins are separated from one another to show, that each of them have their individualization, which is a distinction made by the mind, in order to subordinate the physical to cosmic laws (the black portions of the coins illuminated by the yellow ornaments, are symbols of the universal laws.[59])

The alternating of the flowers and of leaves show a balance between the realizations of the dynamic potentials (the leaves) and that of the animistic riches (the flowers).

The leaves completely surround the four coins in the centre, thus indicating that they form the spiritual quaternary, that computes in part the number 8, while its material quaternary includes the four remaining outer coins, thus symbolizing the entire physical periphery, creating a boundary between two means and one halting to the expansion at the centre of man, with his place in the centre of the card. Here implies transcendence and spirituality.

---

[59] See Three of Coins

The white stems always have their own meaning of synthesis, of active richness and of flowering.

UTILITARIAN MEANINGS IN THE THREE PLANES

MENTAL. This is not a card of luck or happiness, results are exactly equal to and proportionate with the efforts applied. Things do not come by themselves, you have to make an effort to get results.

ANIMISTIC. This card is not sentimental either, but it does provide security in friendship more than in love.

PHYSICAL. By representing proportionate changes, it indicates businesses, that have well established foundations, especially from a commercial point of view.

INVERTED. It brings some disruption to what preceded it.

*

In its elementary sense, the Eight of Coins represents man's deductions, comparing what is above with what is below, proceeding from the known to the unknown, receiving in proportion to what he gives, and having to make an equivalent effort in what he wants to get.

266

NINE OF COINS

SYNTHETIC MEANING

The Nine of Coins, highlights the central coin by means of the surroundings, and places it between two identical quaternaries, which symbolize; that which man has achieved, the balance between his material self and his spiritual self, and where he organizes his knowledge of the material, in order to build his future persona.

ANALYTIC MEANING

The central coin symbolizes man, because this cannot be represented in any other way, then by a central position of the card. The complex leaf formation that surrounds him indicates the nature of his work. When analysing the card, it will be noted, that the two squares of the four coins, are symmetrically arranged and thus show their equivalence in the spiritual and the material on this card, as well as their balance. It can be flipped around without modifying anything.

This balance also reappears in the symmetry of the artwork where only the colours differ. The colours change symmetrically, blue takes the place of red and vice versa. Only the blue corolla on the flower below is replaced in the one on the top, by a yellow colour, to show that it corresponds to the spiritual plane more than to the material plane. If matter needs intelligence to rise upwards, the spirit penetrates the below by sympathy and by intuition and not by reason. This is also why blue replaces yellow in the lower branches.

Translator: The reader might be a little puzzled with Marteau´s text. To understand the symmetry Marteau is writing about here, it may be important to disclose, that Grimaud also publishes a slightly different version of their Ancien Tarot de Marseille; the *Dusserre* edition. This card from the *Dusserre*, is probably what Marteau is referring to in his text on the 9 of Coins. The notable difference with the card shown on the previous page and the one from *Dusserre,* is the red flower replacing the small red chalice and the yellow stem below. This card has been recreated here from the Emrik & Binger.

The yellow coloration bordering the blue chalice of the flower with the red bud, makes the top of the card stand out, while the red chalice and its blue bud implies the material quaternary.

The layout of the line work shows, through the lateral extensions, that surround the central coin, a primitive orientation of man at work, first of all from his "Self", and his understanding of the environment through his psyche and material activities, in order to balance them on the two double crosses in the centre, to experience himself as a flower, or rather as a powerful bud, a symbol of his future being.

UTILITARIAN MEANINGS IN THE THREE PLANES

MENTAL. Extensive knowledge, particularly in cosmogony. Intelligence that applies to big concepts, to philosophy.

ANIMISTIC. Rich in animism, even passionate in its elevated sense: sweet superior feelings, intense love without conflict. Radiance.

PHYSICAL. Businesses that will obtain results, if they are in their beginning or on a path, an assured return. Health that produces activity, drive.

INVERTED. Small material obstructions of what preceded.

*

In its elementary sense, the Nine of Coins represents the extensive, altruistic and balanced work of man, with the perspective of his union with the world.

TEN OF COINS

SYNTHETIC MEANING

By studying the arrangements in the Ten of Coins, that make the 10, they appear under these successive aspects: 3 + 4 + 3, 5 + 5, 4 + 1 + 4 + 1 and 4 + 2 + 4. The card symbolizes the complexity of the game of cosmic forces and the elements that surround man and from which he builds.

ANALYTIC MEANING

10 = 3 + 4 + 3 representing matter (4) framed and sustained by the ternary equilibrium carried out at the top and at the bottom of this card. When 10 indicates a completed cycle, its construction 5 + 5 shows a transition (5) in possibility to another cycle. The repetition of 5 indicates that it could be done both in a material way and in a spiritual way. 4 + 1 with 4 + 1 provides the dominant perspective, because the central coin, which here symbolizes unity, is crossed by the vertical axis and gives rise to extreme outbursts.

Placed inside 4 coins, it denotes an activity in a passivity, and since 10 is a number of synthetic order, it signifies a higher spark, which animates matter or the upper mental faculty above and below the inferior brain. From here everything emanates and from here channels tie in (through the white stem), the reconciliations between the individual and the universal. It symbolizes man´s individuality in the centre through a map of cosmic principles.

The central double cross represents the network of all the complexities of currents, that bring together the centres of forces represented by the coins. The flowers and the buds indicate the evolution in preparation, which will expire or hatch in the following cycles. Diagonal leaves reconcile the different planes because they are fluidic transmissions. The 10 ends the numerical series of the Minor Arcana, providing the following details:

Card 10 implies in the Swords; free will. In the Clubs; the power of work. In the Cups; aspiration for help from the divine. In the Coins; building on a logical foundation. The white, blue and red colours have their usual meaning.

UTILITARIAN MEANINGS IN THE THREE PLANES

MENTAL. Universal spirit, more particularly the erudite knowing of material secrets. In a normal circumstance; indication of going to the bottom of things.

ANIMISTIC. Radiant card, but outside an individualistic sense. Love in a big way, because 10 is a perfection, an exaltation.

PHYSICAL. Health, beauty, physical harmony. Particular issues in business affairs, outside perspectives, such as with a class room. Collective and not individual points of view.

INVERTED. This card is not reversible, brings to mind Arcanum XXI the world.

*

In its elementary sense, the Ten of Coins represents a harmonious totalization, that allows man to penetrate the depths of things and organize them for the good of others.

THE MINOR ARCANA COURTS

INTRODUCTION TO THE COURT
CARDS OF THE MINOR ARCANA

The courts of the Minor Arcana are designed to synthesize the polarity of the numbers in activity and passivity, indicated by odd and even numbers, respectively. On the one hand, they are represented by Knights and Kings, and on the other, by Pages and Queens. Human representation has been used to indicate a higher plane than that of numbers, a plane on which responsibility and freedom takes place in acts.

More abstractly, it can be said that the courts symbolize a synthesis of the qualities of the numbers on a higher plane than that of the four Aces, and that they are an adaptation of unity - the principle of the ten numbers - to the Universal, where man stands.

*

The conscious quaternary, formed by the figures, implies a terrestrial value and an evolutionary value, the first symbolizing the state of man in the physical world, and the second, his need to detach himself from the material to evolve. This is indicated by the quaternary of the Pages, which is different than that of the Knights, which in turn differs from that of the Queens, like the latter from that of the Kings.

*

These figures are characterized as follows: THE PAGE, in its elevated state, is a starting point that represents consciousness, not quite come to life and locked in the immobility of 4, so it is conscious chaos, ready to act, however a potential under pressure. He is also an announcer, and his dress and attributes symbolizes the properties of the announcement. More elementally, it indicates potentiality and prepares for its execution, without having enough strength to act, due to its passivity. The four Pages denote an internal work, since they all indicate passivity, but the internal in the proper meaning of each card. This stands out by the emphasis of its symbol, because each Page is represented in turn by a very long sword, a massive club, a very elongated cup, and by two coins, when no other figure has a double symbol.

*

THE KNIGHT is this chaos coming out of its immobility under the effects of an evolutionary blow. The figure is on horseback and not on foot, thus showing that the principle of the Page has been carried forth to his evolution. It follows then he is not his own master, he cannot lead his horse, if he is not in balance. In the elemental order, he is essentially active. He transmits and acts, following the directives of the Page. To perfect this evolution, the Knight must reach THE QUEEN, who represents spiritualized passivity, as well as wisdom and temperance, because the feminine principle, due to its passivity, keeps the tranquillity and the equilibrium necessary to receive wisdom. A fertilizing principle, therefore creative, and that in its elementary sense, illuminates the contributions of the Knight.

*

The three preceding figures allow for final realization of THE KING, the principle of strength and power, which results from the fusion of the passive element; the Queen, and the active element; the Knight. The King represents domination on all planes, on the cosmic plane, for example, over the elements. In his elementary principle, he is a conductor.

*

The Minor Arcana courts constitute a mixed bag, between Universal laws, which this quaternary obeys, and the laws of matter, which they direct. These cards are therefore placed last, as they are intermediators.

*

The tarot is then three series all relating to the combinations of numbers; the first, formed by the Major Arcana, represents the action of the Universal through the combinations of numbers; the second, formed by the Minor Arcana from 1 to 10, indicate the combinations of the numbers in themselves, and the third, formed by the Minor Arcana Courts, indicate the reactions of man on the combinations of numbers.

THE MINOR ARCANA
THE COURT OF SWORDS

PAGE OF SWORDS

SYNTHETIC MEANING

The Page of Swords, through its figure turned to the left, using his left arm to hold a sword, and with his planted

pose, stresses immobility, demonstrates passivity[60]. A great yellow sword he holds vertically as well as a red sheath, indicating a strong mental action, he detaching from matter to orient himself towards the Above. The whole synthesis shows the preparation of man to detach his mental activities from matter and organize his spiritual force on a higher plane.

ANALYTIC MEANING

The sword symbolizes the extension of a base (the pommel), in an explicit

---

[60] The reader will want to refer to the Page of Cups, the second paragraph of Analytic Meaning and foot note from the Juggler.

direction (the blade), it indicates an extension of an action, whose origin is in matter (red sheath). However, the Page's passivity does not allow this extension to be effective and to engender a manifestation, it makes him instead thread water, meaning, a preparation for a specific future action.

FEATURES BY ANALOGY

The yellow lining of the cape indicates the potential for powers of intelligence. All potentials are dormant and constitutes a kind of envelope of forces, just as the cape envelops man. This yellow also represents a mental action, protected by a spiritual force, implied by the blue, which will assume its powers of manifestation, thanks to a physical force, it being on the shoulders and indicated by the colour of flesh.

The swords blade has a double black central ridge at its base, and merging into one ridge about two thirds up its length, thus underlining the potential for force[61]. Its double ridge and its big pommel indicate, that man has, at the origin of his actions, a mental capacity for double action; which is to say, he can be led to good or evil.

The seven buttons on his tunic signify his affinity with the first seven cards, and in particular with Arcanum VII.

His hat with a wide red brim, lining in blue, shows his dullness of the material, not being able to act without a vibration of spirituality. However, the yellow cap specifies that the intelligence that encourages him and takes him out of this state will come from the Above. His head, tilted to the left, further emphasizes his passivity, and his white hair, his impersonality. He does not direct or influence an effort, he prepares it.

---

[61] See on this subject the explanations given to the Seven of Swords, as well as those for the Three and Five of Swords.

The white of the collar around the neck, the cuff and the cross-guard of the sword, reinforce this notion, signifying a voluntary absence of action, a denial of his person.

His blue legs, finishing in shoes of red and turned in opposite direction, are the indication of a future progression, through the spiritual, currently in a latent state.

The two tufts of grass, one green and the other yellow, emerge from uneven yellow grounds and are contributions of vital and mental energy.

UTILITARIAN MEANINGS IN THE THREE PLANES

MENTAL. Upcoming, events in progress.

ANIMISTIC and PHYSICAL. This card is indifferent in the physical, the blue legs and the red feet indicate little contact with this plane.

INVERTED. Obstruction. Powerlessness in the face of superior forces. Inability to organize mental activities.

*

In sum, in its elementary sense, the Page of Swords represents the inner elaboration that occurs in the mind of man, when he is deciding to act.

KNIGHT OF SWORDS

SYNTHETIC MEANING

This card depicts a knight clad in armour, holding a white sword and mounted on a galloping horse, it flesh-coloured, partly covered in a horse blanket and with its hoofs in blue. In this way, this knight symbolizes a sudden, powerful, enlightened and disciplined, propagative force, which relies on the vital energies of the physical world, which propel him with their animistic qualities.

ANALYTIC MEANING

The blue armour of the Knight of Swords displays an energetic and disciplined will, animistic in nature. The mask that he wears on his left shoulder, is a symbol, that the power granted to this knight is transitory, and that it does not belong to him, it will be removed together with the armour, he must unfasten during rest.

The long sword, no colour, as well as its cross-guard, indicate by their whiteness a synthetic force born of light and, consequently a strong projection towards the higher planes. It also underlines an abstract message, meaning, it does not reveal the plane on which its action has been directed.

FEATURES BY ANALOGY

The blanket that covers the horse, covers it with flexible elements however still material, showing that the point of support and transmission of the knight's force (flesh colour of the horse) is enveloped and protected by the vital energies of the physical.

This blanket, forming a shell, mostly red, with a yellow seam is joined above and below in front by a white band, in this way, expressing that their activity will be intelligent and balanced. The different patterns, arabesque and various black dots, that appear on the yellow parts of the blanket, represent the parts in the material, still in development.

The hoofs which points of contact with the ground, are blue[62], indicate the spiritual base of this progression. The horseshoe of the hoof is fastened with 5 nails[63], 5 being the number of vibration, that is, of the propagation from one state to the other, or from one plane to another. The number 10, symbolized by the 10 nails enforcing the rim of his helmet, (2 x 5) accentuate this idea, but also recall Arcanum X the Wheel of Fortune, because the Knight of Swords contributes, as he relates to his environment, the accentuation of an evolution, or the renewal of events, or more explicit; an unforeseen change of a situation.

---

[62] The hoofs on all the Knight´s horses are blue, signifying the spiritual basis of their action.

[63] This detail is also found in the other three Knights.

The blue of the breastplate and of the helmet shows that the spiritual protects him in his fights, and the yellow, that this protection is based on intelligence.

The white belt, on a blue background of the breast plates, indicates that his spirituality is based on purity. The knight must remain grounded in the spiritual, by his mounting into the blue stirrups with feet in red; also, the yellow of his leg, as he touches the upper part of the stirrup, implying that intelligence must ally itself with the spiritual. The knee pad, blue in front and yellow in the back, confirms the above.

The mane serves the horse in squashing insects, and by appearing in blue here, it implies a spiritual broom, that will remove the parasites, that may want to latch on to his will.

The horse's gallop indicates the nature of the speed of the force propagated by this card. The skewed direction of the horse, indicates a passive orientation of this knight, showing it is not the substance of what he transmits, but rather his rapid trajectory in a committed action. The four blue hoofs signify a spiritual direction.

The flesh-coloured mask that the knight wears on the shoulder, symbolizes the physical inheritance of the fights carried out in the past, at the point of the sword, the destruction and dispel of his flaws, as well as the burdens, that this inheritance imposes on him. It is on the physical plane, he must strike, because the upper part of the arm that holds the sword is red, and his forearm and hand are flesh-coloured.

The uneven yellow soil, streaked with black, indicates resistance. The yellow tufts of grass are assistance in shape of intellectual contributions.

UTILITARIAN MEANINGS IN THE THREE PLANES

MENTAL. Bringing clarity and solution to projects, by revealing unexpectedly their multiple facets.

ANIMISTIC. Change, quick contribution, vibrant, since the horse is galloping.

PHYSICAL. Unforeseen realizations, not expected.

INVERTED. Great impediments, disputes, setback in business.

*

In short, in its elementary sense, the Knight of Swords represents the quick command by man, his aptitude for decision making, prior to an unexpected event and that make up destiny unforeseen.

QUEEN OF SWORDS

SYNTHETIC MEANING

Represented by a woman turned to the left, with white hair, crowned, sitting on a wide and tall throne and holding a red sword vertically. The Queen of Swords symbolizes the almighty role played by intuition, enlightened in judgment, to which mental activities must be subordinated, when exercised in the material world.

ANALYTIC MEANING

The queens signify passivity, of subconscious intuition, meaning mental and animistic assimilation, allowing enlightened and inspired understanding, because they all wear crowns and have white hair spread over their shoulders, the only exception being the Queen of Coins.

The crown, whose shape indicates a radiation, takes its origin in the subtle planes, and through its rosettes, centres of attraction, constitutes a reflection of cosmic principles and show, that the queens have access to the Universal.

The white hair represents a complex and a synthetized radiance of the mental, while its spread curls denotes a great force of will, without predominance of one side over the other, meaning, the left pole over the right, and vice versa.

The passivity of the queens is indicated by their sitting position, and, with the exception of the Queen of Clubs, by their orientation to the left. The seat of the Queen of Swords is more boldly indicated, because her incubation is deeper than that of the other queens, and it is reinforced by the necessary involvement of her dress, that is, she is compelled to work more from within.

In short, her pose and what accompanies her underline the mental particularities of this card.

FEATURES BY ANALOGY

The sword she holds shows that her role is to judge, because the sword slits, splits, symbolizing judgment, and this must be impersonal and inspired by a synthetic view, as the white hair of the queen defines it.

This sword is red, because solutions on a matter, are called for, and its cross-guard is yellow, to show that intelligence must intervene, in order to avoid taking judgment slave to matter. Her gaze turned to the red sword, to the left, also indicates that she must immerse herself in her passive side, that is, in her knowledge of the physical, to elaborate on the elements underpinning her decision.

The points indicated on the rim of the crown, the collar and the belt evoke their agreement with the cosmic principles and their affinity with the Major Arcana represented by these numbers. Those of the crown, numbering 12, link it with the first 12 Arcana and make this card more active, when it is with one of them. Furthermore, the number 12 forms a complete evolutionary cycle, and a judgment is only well established, if it embraces the whole evolution of the issue.

The 8 points on the collar and the belt show their affinity with Arcanum VIII, and share similar qualities with Justice; but as this card belongs to the Minor Arcana, that is, to the elemental principles, its action is less broad, less extensive, less powerful and less concrete than that of Arcanum VIII. The points of the collar are in the sense of animistic justice, and those of the belt, in the sense of practical justice.

UTILITARIAN MEANINGS IN THE THREE PLANES

MENTAL. Judgement obtained through intuition.

ANIMISTIC. Being emotional protective in an intimate sense and the consequences resulting from that.

PHYSICAL. No action, since arising from the mind its passivity prevents it from bringing change, for example in litigation. In business, it does not contribute anything. In case of health; it indicates, the doctor or remedy acts for the best, however without being able to produce results.

INVERTED. Very bad, because it implies injustice, bad judgment and slander.

*

In its elementary sense, the Queen of Swords represents the obligation for man not to act without having consulted his intuition, awakening through concentration, the knowledge of his mental activities about the subject matter at hand.

KING OF SWORDS

ROY. D EPEE

SYNTHETIC MEANING

Holding in his right hand a sword, whose blade is flesh-coloured, and in his left a baton of command, wearing a hat, with a white interior, blue and red exterior, with a crown-shaped cap, the head turned to the right, and in a half-seated position, the King of Swords indicates the preparation for clear cut action, made with superior knowledge, of mental activity.

ANALYTIC MEANING

The parts that appear in white in the King of Swords indicate, firstly, his impersonality and, without specifying any special action, reveal a state of consciousness in man, properly adapted to the work implied by the calls of evolution. In other words, an impregnation of light into the intimate organization of the part of his conceptions linked to the Universal (white interior of the hat), to his mental activity (white hair), to the balance of his desires with his physical operations (white belt) and in the direction of his actions (white baton).

FEATURES BY ANALOGY

The king is turned to the left, his head to the right, and he is sitting with one foot forward; meaning, he is passive and stable, but he is ready for action.

The sword is flesh-coloured, showing that the king's action is exercised through vital drive and extends to humanity; meaning, he clothes himself with altruism; he encourages things presented to him. The cross-guard, big and yellow, symbolizes the intelligence in this activity.

Furthermore, on the knee on which the sword rests, the circle that appears is related to activity, just as the two circles on the other knee are related to passivity. When they meet, these circles reinforce their effects with one another.

His white baton of command, striped in black, signifies the dominance of his subconscious, because it is held by the left hand, and thus indicates, that the king does not have the concerns of acting outside his will. The black stripes indicate, that his impersonality is aligned with divine impersonality, which is absolute. The gold pommel is similar to that of the sword.

The wavy hat, specifies that the mental constructions of the king put him in a relationship with cosmic infinity. The crown, inside the hat and partly covered, shows that, when manifesting in part, changes take place spontaneously between the cosmic elements and the subconscious knowledge of the mind.

The two different shoulder masks, indicate his actions in opposite planes, seen by the contrast in their expressions.

The 12 twines of the belt meet the 12 Major Arcana, pointing out the balance between these 12 principles in the animistic and the physical. These are similar to the points on the belt of the Queen of Swords, but where hers were points of abstractions, and were associated with the intimate and profound fabric of the Major Arcana, the twines here are adapted to the kings more practical aspects.

The other points that appear on his dress are the centres of fluidic condensations, that manifest the actions of the king on the different planes, matching the parts of the clothing on where they are found, and the meanings are indicated by the number of points: The 4 points placed under the mask on the left, imply his role in the quaternary of the elements, that is to say, in matter. The 6 points on the left breastplate, show what must be made to evolve through sacrifice of the psyche or his evolutionary animistic role, and the 8 on the right breastplate, where he must make and evolve through the fairness of his judgments.

The chair on which the king is seated is flesh-coloured, with a yellow edge, part of which is grooved with black lines, also mirrored under his feet, evoking the karmic shadows, that accompany the certainty of death, as well as the resistances to overcome on the material plane.

The black lines traced below on the chair show the work of the material world, based on the knowledge of the past. The chair made of matter, serves as a support, it brings this benefit to an inner work. This pattern is made up of a spiral and leaves, thus indicating that this work is manifested through the geometric laws applied to the evolution of matter or of nature, since the spiral is an extension of force (nebulous), and the leaves are an expansion of vegetative life.

The black colour indicates its hidden role and the karmic darkness that can flow from it.

The mask on his left shoulder, surrounded and framed by black lines, seems to laugh, on the right, the mask without lines has its mouth closed. They are the two sides of a matter, the one on the right represents activity of the psyche, and the one on the left recalls, with its stretch marks, the fatality that weighs on the King of Swords.

The set of clothing, analogous to that of the character in the Chariot, corresponds to a setting out on a road and to an energy of the psyche, reinforcing his mental activities, typical for the swords.

UTILITARIAN MEANINGS IN THE THREE PLANES

MENTAL. Rich, complex contribution, characterized by the importance of playing the right role. His judgment is balanced and deep. Influences all domains. Ease in taking stock, to give solutions to different things (action specified by the two shoulder masks).

ANIMISTIC. Protection and reassurance.

PHYSICAL. This card is related to major Arcana V, VI and VIII. A matter wakes him up from his sleep. Questionable health, because of the black flower on the chair, indicating a danger that lurks from the past. In other words, the black lines on the chair, are shadows of which the flower is the result, and the part shaped as 9 is an element that stands out, a disaggregation from the past. A certain fatality is associated with this card.

INVERTED. The heaviness of this massive throne, entails temperament, coarseness, low pleasures.

*

In short, in its elementary sense, the King of Swords represents the achievements of man in all tendencies of his mental activities, when this tendency is accompanied by reflection.

THE MINOR ARCANA
THE COURT OF CUPS

PAGE OF CUPS

SYNTHETIC MEANING

The Page of Cups, through the orientation of his march, the large open cup, he presents up front, and his white hair, crowned with four-petal flowers, indicates that all work, of the psyche or spiritual effort, accompanied by an offering, becomes an announcer or transmitter of a beneficial contribution.

VALET·DE·COUPE

ANALYTIC MEANING

The passivity of the cup, together with that of the Page, is indicated by the march to the left. In the absence of initiative, the page remains immobile, therefore, his movement indicates, that he is internal and that his march symbolizes a trend and not a reality.

In other words, it should be remembered that his movement only takes place to the left for the reader of the card, and that, for the page on the card, the movement is made to his right.[64] This contradiction is apparent. The activity of the page coming from the right is within and implies strong internal elaboration. In its external manifestation, this activity reverses its meaning, like the gesture of a person seen in a mirror, and this transposition symbolizes a strong psychological tendency, strong due to the internal operations of the page, which is altruistic, since it takes place from the right, and an aspect of the psyche, since appearing on the outside as an expansion of the heart.

FEATURES BY ANALOGY

The cup, long and narrow, indicates the depth and measure of what it contains. It is open so that it can be filled, indicating with this, that anything should be given in exchange for the promise made by the march of the page, in order for there to be a communion.

He has the cup in his right hand and the lid in his left hand, to show that man encloses or discovers his achievements according to the needs of his efforts.

The red prominence in the centre of the cup, shows that this offering must be a sacrifice made in the material.

On top of the cup, the veil, flesh-coloured, from the back of a yellow fabric that surrounds the neck, a protection that provides an intelligent conception and a use of vital forces, since the gifts of the psyche, foundational to the page is necessarily balanced and must be protected from any expiration.

Furthermore, these offerings, half-veiled and frankly undiscovered, are hopes, ongoing promises, therefore possibilities and not yet realities.

---

[64] See the explanations on poses of the figures presented, in card the Juggler.

The wide red tunic, floating around the figure, not tightly enclosed as in the Page of Swords, shows him more detached from the material.

The flower crown indicates, that the mental elaborations of the contributions or of the receptivity of the cup are of an emotional nature, but capable of becoming affective feelings. The four petals imply the concretization symbolized by the quaternary.

The whiteness of the hair shows the impersonality of the page, that is, the absence of individualism at the dawn of the work of the psyche.

Red shoes indicate work on the lower planes.

The black striations and the uneven yellow soil symbolizes resistance in all planes. The green tufts of grass, contributions of vital energy to be overcome, and the yellow tufts, intellectual contributions.

While the cup cards from two to ten represent entirely yellow cups, with the exception of the red top, which symbolizes the receptacle of human activities and passionate feelings clothed with intelligence, and if launched with a sincere spirit towards the Above, will be successful. The Page of Cup has a red sphere[65] in the centre, which implies the energetic efforts, that the soul must make in matter, to reconcile the universal and synthetic side of animistic intelligence, manifested by the sphere.

UTILITARIAN MEANINGS IN THE THREE PLANES

MENTAL. Comfort in spiritual thoughts, in affairs. Ruling out doubt.

---

[65] The same detail exists for the Knight of Cups and the Queen of Cups.

ANIMISTIC. Relief more powerful, than what preceded it, because the cups are psychological comforts of hope. Emotional support.

PHYSICAL. Complete detachment from an emotional issue, release from sadness. Health; hope of a cure, if there is serious illness.

INVERTED. Overwhelmed by distress, mental destitution. Feeling of total abandonment.

*

In short, in its elementary sense, the Page of Cups represents the spiritual and happy contribution, that comes to man, when his evolution of the psyche is accompanied by an offering of the soul.

KNIGHT OF CUPS

SYNTHETIC MEANING

The Knight of Cups, head bare, supporting, in his right hand, a wide-open cup and trotting to the left, indicates the enthusiastic impulse of man called upwards and drawn into altruistic expansion.

ANALYTIC MEANING

The Knight of Cups signifies a promise of contribution in exchange for an offering. The rider arrives with this contribution, animistic in nature, first of all by virtue of the innate significance of the cup, and second because he is turned to the left.

CAVALIER·DE·COUPE

FEATURES BY ANALOGY

This knight has the appearance of a page on horseback. The cup, which is placed flat on his right hand like in the Page of Cups, symbolizes the accumulated earthly treasures, meaning, all of human wisdom; but these treasures, which can lead the possessor of the cup astray, are transitory, wisdom being unable to crystallize in a state of immobility.

When the cup is in the shape of a double ended trumpet it can be turned on its head, and the wisdom, it contains in a passive, unconscious state, can be oriented both upwards and downwards, for both good and for bad. The cup of the knight breaks this symmetry, its top is wider, to show that the treasures of wisdom in its possession can no longer change their qualities; they remain good or bad.

His head, without a hat, and the open cup are the indications, that he is directly receiving inspiration and support from Above.

The horse, flesh-coloured, symbolizes the nervous energy and the vital forces of the support. The trot marks the impetus and shows, that these forces could exceed the power of the knight, if he does not hold back with the reigns, held with the left hand, thus indicating that he cannot direct it completely, only restrain it.

The red sphere in the centre of the cup has the same significance as that of the Page of Cups, the efforts that the soul must make in the material.

The blue mane, as well as the four hoofs, have the same significance as in the Knight of Swords.

The four points on the horse's breast collar correspond to the quaternary and Arcanum IV the Emperor, and signify the powerful strength of the contribution, as well as its solidity; the 4 points and the 3 points on the rump strap show, that the knight acts on the 3 planes of

298

consciousness[66] and under the 4 constitutive aspects of the material plane; meaning, with a large foot print (3 + 4 = 7 = the range).

The yellow ornaments, that decorate the horse, show that intelligence is at the base of its action, and the stirrup, that the knight's point of support is neutral; knowledge is not contained, it goes from one place to another, it spreads.

The variety of the colours on the dress has the same significance as in the Knight of Clubs. The meaning of the ground is the same as in the Knight of Swords.

UTILITARIAN MEANINGS IN THE THREE PLANES

MENTAL. Contribution of fertile ideas, inspiration, ideas that arise spontaneously.

ANIMISTIC. Outburst of artistic gifts, especially for a musician, because the scale is represented by 4 + 3 = 7.

PHYSICAL. Happy marriages, good match, very good health.

INVERTED. The power of the card is only reduced in half, being too active for the effects to be extinguished; there are delays or impediments.

*

In its elementary sense, the Knight of Cups represents the sensitive and affective part of man, susceptible to generous expressions and devotion.

---

[66] Translator: Marteau defines the planes of consciousness as; Spirituality, Intelligence and Superior Mentality. See Arcanum XI Strength.

REYNE DE COUPE

QUEEN OF CUPS

SYNTHETIC MEANING

Seated to the left, under a canopy, and wearing a double headdress, holding in her right hand a closed cup, and in her left hand a sceptre in the shape of a white spindle, the Queen of Cups symbolizes intimate condensations of animistic forces, in order to express them in the form of love in its universality, both in devotion and in affection, and with the feeling of its daily application.

ANALYTIC MEANING

The cup, resting on her right knee and being firmly held by the right hand, denotes its capacity for achievements in the material world, in its full animistic radiance.

The canopy, due to its enveloping shape, and the double headdress with the closed cup and its spherical shape, show the great passivity of the cup, further accentuated by the orientation to the left. It is concentrated within man, yet also has universality, the sphere being the representation of the universe as a whole.

This is also indicated by the shape of the sceptre, whose white colour, symbolizes the abstract and the synthesis of principles, constituting a condensing antenna of universal forces. These are collected at the base by the left hand, which transmits them to the psyche of man.

FEATURES BY ANALOGY

The spindle in general symbolizes daily work, accompanied with perseverance. This aspect, in addition to the previous one, signifies the application of feelings, represented by the Queen of Cups in the concrete, and in the details of life. They represent the thousand shades of love, that her material side make noble. The colour, flesh and yellow, of the canopy, further illustrates this voluntary descent into life and intelligence of matter.

The red seam in front, that allows for communication from the neck of the Queen of Cups to the grip of the spindle, with her hand representing an active current, allows force of action in the physical. The spindle acting as the antenna.

The belt, with its 9 points, evokes the triple ternary, that is, the harmonious agreement of all the worlds, on the 3 planes. These points also indicate the complexity of the domains, where activity of the psyche can be exercised, because the 9 implies the end of the primordial numbers.

The blue headdress, adorned with a red disk, sandwiched between the hair and the crown, indicates a will, not to open up to the Universal (the crown signifying radiance in the Universal) before having contemplated the works of good in the material, impregnated with sacrifice and conceived with a material spirit (the red of the headdress is wrapped in blue).

The red sphere, which separates the tetrahedral foot of the cup from its spherical upper part, symbolizes, due to the Queen of Cups´ capacity for diffusion and owing to her particular intelligent nature, her energetic, voluntary and incessant effort, the work of the soul in matter. It is the work of reconciling the universal with that of the synthetic role of animistic intelligence, manifested through the sphere, with its structure on the physical plane, symbolized by the tetrahedron.

The closed cup reinforces its initial passivity and accentuates the animistic condensation implied by this card, which is expressed through the treasures of love, that every being deep down can possess, but an effort is necessary in order to open it, implied in the use of her right hand in holding this cup.

There are three rectangles on the upper part of the cup, that represent the ternary on the spiritual plane; love, light and life, and the six motifs in the form of Greek fret, in the centre, indicate the double ternary; light love, life under its double aspect of passivity and activity.

The eight lines below symbolize the four states of matter in the passive and active, and the three lines on the central red sphere, are the reflections of the ternary on the material plane.

UTILITARIAN MEANINGS IN THE THREE PLANES

MENTAL. Transcendence. Getting in touch with universal forces or with great intelligence.

ANIMISTIC. This card is elevated over passionate love. It represents universal love and superior altruism.

PHYSICAL. Mastery, complete success, all emotional affairs are fully realized. Perfect health.

INVERTED. Very bad. Persistent obscuration, because all principles are turned upside down. Complete misguidance. The assistance, in this case, will be rendered by the Page of Swords, and especially by the Knight of Swords.

*

In its elementary sense, the Queen of Cups represents the feeling of altruism, that man carries deep within, which he can only manifest through the daily efforts of devotion and affection.

KING OF CUPS

SYNTHETIC MEANING

Well seated, with the body oriented to the left and the head to the right, wearing a crown, broadly extended both to the right and left, blue in the interior and red on the exterior, holding with his right hand a tall cup with a small opening, the King of Cups shows, that all effective manifestations must be accompanied by a passive state, that allows man to orient himself to the above by the extension of his psyche, such as in prayer or any other means of mystical elevation.

ANALYTIC MEANING

The protrusions of the crown signify animistic outbursts, thrusts of energy born of feelings to open up to the universal, and characterize a great activity of the psyche with a very impersonal feeling.

304

FEATURES BY ANALOGY

The crown, solidly placed on his head, covering it completely, shows that the extent of its radiance embraces his whole mind and allows him to communicate directly with the universal.

The white headdress, under the crown, is a synthetic element interspersed to establish a transition between the mental and its means of expression (crown and wings). The part that covers his ear forms a protection to avoid the mixing of external currents and shows, that he is not allowed to be distracted in his mission. The black lines that appear in it have their own resistance, and the white fabric that extends from his neck to the cup indicates the impersonality, that, in the end, synthesizes his contribution. His moustache, also white, and his beard split into two, shows the impartiality of his judgment.

The king's well-established position is intended to affirm the passivity imposed on him by the nature of the cup, but his head directed to the right, indicates the obligation of an activity within, which is affirmed by the fact that the cup is held by his right hand.

The cup is elongated, to emphasize the time of incubation of altruistic or mystical feelings and the extension of that, man must give to himself. The cup of the Page was equally tall, but contributing only hope, he should be receiving rather than giving.

The Page and the Knight only support their cups, while the King and Queen hold it firmly indicating, that the first two courts receive; the Page to hatch, the Knight to transmit; while the second court pair; the Queen, a force of capture that ensures intuition, and the King, a force of diffusion, who makes manifest his psyche.

The left hand, placed on a golden belt, implies an inner effort to achieve a mental balance between the conscious (chest) and the instinctive (belly) sentiments. The four buttons on his blue tunic indicate the four planes of elevation, going from that of psyche to the spiritual, through animism and the mental.

The red of the cape represents his physical activity, and the yellow seam and lining, the intelligence of this activity, oriented towards fulfillment of the psyche. The black stripes represent the resistances he encounters.

The lower part of the throne, flesh-coloured, with its numerous black stripes, represents the obstacles that the king encounters in the nervous domain, before materializing in the physical, his contribution by the psyche underlined by the blue on his feet.

The yellow floor, curiously enhanced with black lines in every way, confirms his passivity.

UTILITARIAN MEANINGS IN THE THREE PLANES

MENTAL Safety in judgement.

ANIMISTIC. Very extensive love, very comforting (as a Saint Vincent de Paul), very dynamic as a feeling. Protection by the psyche.

PHYSICAL. Related to the two Major Arcana XVII and XXI. Abundance. Significant affairs, which go well, with social or public importance, such as an international exhibition.

INVERTED. Very heavy and difficult, with great difficulties in release, obtained only after a long time.

*

In its elementary sense, the King of Cups represents the voluntary renunciation of personal will, to confidently open up to the Universal.

THE MINOR ARCANA
THE COURT OF CLUBS

PAGE OF CLUBS

SYNTHETIC MEANING

The Page of Clubs, by his orientation to the right, his left foot forward, ready to march, his two hands on a vertical green club, ready to be used, implies a tension in his passivity and an activity close to physical, implying a source of energy. The indication; the forces of nature are at the disposal of man and always ready to be used by him.

ANALYTIC MEANING

The green cane, in the shape of a club, indicates the vital energies that man will use as support, as a lever, as a hammer, or as a subtle force, through fire. The hands of the page, posing without sign of subjugation, indicates an awareness of those forces, and the space between them, show activity and power in all domains, as his hold on the club is absolute.

VALET DEBATON·

The red cap of the page denotes, that his work is organized on the physical plane, with an intelligent crown and with an impersonality, indicated by the two bands, one yellow and the other white.

FEATURES BY ANALOGY

The green of the club means, that matter can only produce fruit when it takes on a state of consciousness. Its shape, wider towards the ground, symbolizes that matter will always be heavier, but that it will have, for those who know how to use it, a very solid base and will become his servant in all things. It could, likewise, be the instrument of man´s destruction, depending on its use.

The red mantle, lined with yellow, which he wears over his blue tunic with blue and flesh sleeves, symbolizes the forces of nature, that only cease to be active once man penetrates into his spiritual domain. Consequently, if he enters there, these forces will no longer be manageable. Therefore, in order to use them he needs to cover himself with a red mantle (matter), but he must not forget, when handling them, to be internally dressed with spirituality (blue).

The bare legs remind us that those forces, which can serve man in his journey, will not, bring him anything that he can build on. He will be naked, because these forces do not give anything in the pure spiritual domain and therefore do not help his evolution.

The black lines, on the yellow ground (mental), on the blue tunic (spiritual) and on the flesh of the legs (physical action), as well as the white hair curls (impersonality), represent the resistances in matter, but the tufts of green grass and the green club is the pledge of energy, that will allow him to triumph over these obstacles.

UTILITARIAN MEANINGS IN THE THREE PLANES

MENTAL. Things brought onsite, ready to be used. Put in form, something that clearly will take shape.

ANIMISTIC. An imminent union prepares for its manifestation, its physical realization.

PHYSICAL. On to the next activity (the Page has the club and is willing to use it). Health recovered. Start-up of a business in preparation. It will go from planning to a material state.

INVERTED. Delay. Confusion in recently completed projects.

*

In short, in its elementary sense, the Page of Clubs indicates the fermentation of the material energies available to man and that incite him to act.

KNIGHT OF CLUBS

SYNTHETIC MEANING

Richly dressed, mounted on a trotting horse, whose white head is turned to the left, the Knight of Clubs, holding his club in his left hand, indicates a strong passivity and inner work, but as he carries his club on the card´s right and vertically, it nevertheless implies, he manifests the energy of which he is a transmitter, and that he represents the transport of these physical energies through matter, until they hatch.

ANALYTIC MEANING

The Page of Clubs symbolized the energies, that nature makes available to man, enclosed in matter, but can only be used after some hatching work. All the forces used by man undergo preparatory work, before being put into play; such as the slow processing of coal, chemicals, minerals from deposits, etc.

In the Knight of Clubs, this internal elaboration is indicated by the horse, an organized force, but without personal action, because its head is white, and if its blue mane implies energy, in the spiritual. However, its horse blanket, flesh-coloured, hinders it by enveloping it in matter, since still woven from vital forces, ensures the activity of its internal work. The immobility of the horse shows the passivity necessary for this internal work. It also constitutes a basis that provides the certainty, that things are going to settle down on the physical plane.

The push of energy through matter to rise to a higher plane, is indicated by the vertical direction of the club and its elevated position.

FEATURES BY ANALOGY

In opposition to the page leaning on his club in rough ground, thus symbolizing the man ready to journey on in his terrestrial life, the Knight of Clubs, through the progression evoked by his horse, represents the man heading towards his evolution.

The horse's head is turned on its side and its legs are hidden, to indicate that the man in his physical life is ignorant and should not know in advance, where his steps will take him; however, the visible, blue-coloured hoofs, show that he surely is guided by a spiritual force. The appearance of the horse, his intelligent air, with pointed ears, and his blue mane denotes, that the abstract plane is not inattentive to the physical plane.

The yellow club and its red upper end means that man, having started by walking awkwardly in matter, now takes his strength (symbol of the club) and walks with the intelligence of the Above, ever in contact with matter, but not led by it. The knight looks attentively at his club, because his gaze, a symbol of intelligent effluvia, turns towards the symbol of strength.

His hat, in the shape of an ∞, shows by the arrangement of colours; blue, yellow and red, that the elaboration of forces is made in balance under the impulse of animism, clothed with intelligence, expressing itself in the physical through mental activities.

The wealth of his clothes determines the amount of knowledge acquired through successive lives, and his general appearance, the mastery, man can acquire by drawing inspiration from the forces up above.

The 4 points on the apron, as well as the 4-petalled flower on the knee, indicate the material work of the knight, while the 7 points[67] on the breast collar, show that the work of the energies is done in all its forms, because the septenary symbolizes all vibrational scales. These numbers also establish a link between the Knight of Clubs and the Emperor (Arcanum IV), as well as the Chariot (Arcanum VII).

The stirrup, flesh-coloured[68], underlines that the support lever, that allows this ascent, this evolution, is in a physical plane, and the red strap[69] is the skittish support of physical activity.

The same meaning from the ground as in Knight of Swords

---

[67] Translator: Please note that the Grimaud shows 8 points.

[68] Translator: Please note that the current Grimaud shows the stirrup in white. Older decks from Grimaud have depicted the stirrup in flesh colour.

[69] Translator: Please note that the current Grimaud shows the strap in flesh colour. Older decks from Grimaud have depicted the strap in red.

UTILITARIAN MEANINGS IN THE THREE PLANES

MENTAL. Intelligent and intuitive activity in the material, happy accomplishments.

ANIMISTIC. Reconciliations in matters of feelings of all kind; friendship, affection, association. Protective activity; things kept hidden to allow for an easier incubation.

PHYSICAL. Harmonious accomplishments. Success in business. Happy resolution of an ongoing matter. From the point of view of health; hope for the convalescent to regain his health, of a fresh start in life.

INVERTED. Delay, resistance.

*

In short, in its elementary sense, the Knight of Clubs represents the incubation by man of the material energies made available to him, in order for him to manage them at his convenience.

REYNE DF BASTON·

QUEEN OF CLUBS

SYNTHETIC MEANING

Seated and neatly wrapped up, the Queen of Clubs, facing to the right with her club shaped sceptre, her crown resting on long, loose white hair that cover her shoulders, represents the intimate grouping of the energies of man to ensure dominance over matter and the defence against adverse forces, that may ensue.

ANALYTIC MEANING

The active concern of the Queen of Clubs, to face an unforeseen circumstance, is indicated through her observing gaze turned to the right, and her dominance, by the size of her club.

FEATURES BY ANALOGY

The interposition of the braided hair, between the head and the crown, reduces its radiance and shows, that its dominance is exercised somewhat downwards rather than upwards. The red dress, with a flesh-coloured lining, which covers her completely, is also an indication of her activity in the physical, and the yellow seam is an indication of her intelligence on the different planes oriented towards the material.

Being feminine and passive, she cannot act, and therefore is sitting, with the club resting on her shoulder, as she gathers her strength internally, as determined by the gesture she makes with her left hand by her knee, drawing back her dress. She wears a blue dress, in order to cover, to protect herself from an external attack, and in order to concentrate. This dress indicates the psychological reserves, that she has and the nature of attack could be both an affliction and adverse circumstances.

The tall throne of the Queen of Swords is replaced by a lower throne, barely visible, to show that, she being more material, does not rest as much on that of the higher planes.

The belt, which role is to support and adjust the middle section of the body, indicates through its 7 points, that it can indeed vibrate in the 7 states of matter.[70]

The black stripes, in different directions on the ground, show the imperfections of the material world, of which it has its base, and symbolize the resistances, the obstacles and the difficulties, that man faces in his work with energies in the material world.

---

[70] Solid, liquid, gas, to which is added the four etheric states.

UTILITARIAN MEANINGS IN THE THREE PLANES

MENTAL. Absolute confidence in business from the point of view of competence and success.

ANIMISTIC. Protection in cases of discord, of disunity. Confidence is reborn, because of the dress covering her knees, indicating her protective strength.

PHYSICAL. Great internal energy, preservation in business and in health.

INVERTED. Things weighing you down, confusion and vulgarity because of their nature, difficulty in freeing yourself from circumstances.

*

In its elementary sense, the Queen of Clubs represents the grouping of intimate forces, that man above all, must achieve to ensure his conquest over material energies and to protect himself from their reactions.

KING OF CLUBS

SYNTHETIC MEANING

Dressed in a rich military outfit and wearing a wide hat that encircles a crown, the King of Clubs, who directs his sceptre toward the earth with a firm hand, with his left hand placed near the waist and his knee raised, signifies that the material achievements can only be achieved through precise, balanced and firmly executed work.

ANALYTIC MEANING

The military appearance of the King of Clubs is intended to show that his work is surrounded by energy. His white hair designates his internal balance. The heavy sceptre, clearly directed by the right hand towards the ground, indicates that this character, in order to obtain the achievements, that are incumbent upon him as King, must master situations and clear doubts by resolving things in the concrete.

FEATURES BY ANALOGY

The white sceptre pointing down not resting on the ground, striated with skewed black stripes, and at its white top has a yellow sphere, equally striped in black, and at its base a big yellow ornament, is the expression of power of the king over the material, and although the king wants to act impartial, the obstacles to overcome in his way are numerous.

Under the cuirass, a blue skirt, of the same colour as the breastplates, represent the fluidic rays, that originate from below. On the shoulders, yellow pauldrons, indicating a fluid radiance emanating from above, thus demonstrating, that the powers of man radiate both upwards and downwards.

Against the base of the cuirass, his left hand, meaning passive, one finger pointing to the 4 points on the cuirass, while the forearm rests on a bent knee, means that the interior work of his active thoughts, seek balance (belt), and are exercised in various ways and extend to the 4 planes of matter.[71]

The 14 points, which appear on his clothing, determine this extension. Their symmetrical positions, relative to the centre line of the cuirass, indicate that they are polarized, and that they represent 7 x 2. The 7 gives the range of all vibrations, and its polarization implies, that they occur internally, like sound, and externally, such as through the colours.

The hat, wavy and of symmetrical shape, unlike that of the King of Cups, shows the personal and direct activity of the King of Clubs in the physical, internally blue while externally red, and with the position of a crown on top, specifies that this activity is not the main element of his mental efforts, but includes a balancing of the internal, more specifically a work of the psyche, before being

---

[71] Solid, liquid, gas and etheric, recognizing the final 4 states.

clothed with matter, and that this will then extend widely to both the active and passive worlds. The black stripes on the hat represent the forces of inertia, that the king with his physical activity, will have to overcome.

The raised heel, as with the shadow it casts, make him stand out. This indicates that the immobility of the king is only momentary, and that he will set out, when there is need for it. Meaning that his achievements are not a function of duration but of preparation, work that can suddenly reach their maturity.

The base of the throne, with black lines, show the resistance encountered by the King of Clubs in establishing his actions, and the base plate of the throne, resting on that flesh-coloured square, says action is physical. The yellow legs, the blue post, crowned by a white ball, the yellow part of the seat on which the king is seated, as well as the yellow base rim on the floor where his feet rest, carefully avoiding the colour flesh in the centre, represents the forces that have been granted to him in order to overcome the resistance, that he will find in these planes, where he must act intelligently.

UTILITARIAN MEANINGS IN THE THREE PLANES

MENTAL. Soundness of judgment, for businesses; clarity in the research of things that require energy. Decision.

ANIMISTIC. Spirit of conquest, of enterprise. Influx of material energy. Procreation.

PHYSICAL. Entrepreneur in business. Excellent health. Light but generous nature.

INVERTED. This card, directing the heat of its energy towards matter becomes bad: drunkenness, debauchery due to excess energy expended in pleasure.

320

*

In short, in its elementary sense, the King of Clubs represents the necessity of effort and firm determination in action for success on the material plane.

THE MINOR ARCANA
THE COURT OF COINS

PAGE OF COINS

SYNTHETIC MEANING

The Page of Coins, wearing a hat in the shape of ∞, with a falling brim, firmly positioned on green grounds, holding up high a coin in his right hand and the other on his belt, while another coin appears on the ground close to his right foot, he manifests an elaboration capable of connecting mental states with material states, through fruitful production in the domains of the physical world.

ANALYTIC MEANING

The link between the high and the low results from the extreme positions of the two coins. The one below is not supported by the page, because it is not this figure who raises a matter up to intelligence, rather he is the one who brings it down to the physical. The ∞ shape hat, with a lowered brim pointing to the ground, accentuates, even more, this action of the page, but in an intellectual way. His mediating role is also deduced from the hand, that touches the yellow belt with 4 triangles, splitting the top body from the bottom, thus indicating the intelligent effort being exercised in complete balance between the upper part of matter, represented by the red torso, and its lower part, indicated by the legs. The final equilibrium results from 3, conciliatory equilibria, repeated 4 times, with 4 being the equilibrium of matter.

The passivity of the page is indicated by his immobility, but the action of his right hand in holding the coin, shows that this passivity contains a desire, and is an announcer of achievements to come, since the right side, symbolizes the external efforts of man.[72]

FEATURES BY ANALOGY

The hat in the shape of ∞ also indicates that time does not exist, due to the permanence of the equilibrium represented by the ∞ and the gaze fixed on the coin elevated implies a persistent vigilance. The variety of colours mean, that the action is exerted into all planes. The tufts of green grass on the flesh-coloured ground, indicate a physical contribution of nervous inflow, and the yellow tufts, a mental contribution, in order to fight against the inertia of matter represented by the black lines.

UTILITARIAN MEANINGS IN THE THREE PLANES

MENTAL. Intelligence directed, that is, knowing how to choose the necessary elements for a manifestation.

---

[72] See the information on the Pages in the Introduction to the court cards of the Minor Arcana.

ANIMISTIC. Choosing the necessary elements in order to reach some end.

PHYSICAL. Balance in business and in health.

INVERTED. It is neutralized, since the binding agent no longer exists and its action becomes inoperative.

*

In its elementary sense, the Page of Coins presents himself to man, as a messenger, announcing the manifestation of his projects, because he has conceived them in agreement with the high and the low.

KNIGHT OF COINS

SYNTHETIC MEANING

Mounted on a walking horse, entirely flesh-coloured, and heading to the right, the Knight of Coins, with a club over the shoulder and looking at the coin placed in front of him in eye height, symbolizes the putting into balance of constructive activities, through the certainty of their action, in their advance and with the perfect orientation of their directives.

ANALYTIC MEANING

The coin, placed above, that is to say, in the spiritual region, clearly before the eyes of the knight, is like a star fixed in its direction and towards which he fares calmly. The coin also represents his efforts in the world.

The club, well supported on his shoulder, and since it is in the right hand, confirms his self-assurance and symbolizes his will and his individual energy.

The Knight of Coins has no incubation period. Like the Page of Coins, he has received the message (the page presents the coin with his right hand, he carries it calmly and with the required energy).

FEATURES BY ANALOGY

The Knight of Coins, with the idea of progression evoked by his horse, also symbolizes the transformation of the worlds, and the yellow club, held in his right hand, indicates their inevitable intelligent destruction on the physical plane.

His activity is drawn only from the vital forces, since the horse is flesh-coloured, with the exception being the blue hoofs, indicate the need to bring his support to the animistic level (see Knight of Swords). The walk of the horse indicates a certain advance, but calm and a measured effort. The orientation to the right confirms his resolve in his activity.

He rides in the opposite direction of the other knights, having turned around to underscore clearly, that his path is opposite to that which has been carved for others, towards paths that yield results, his is completely isolated and he has no concerns for the thoughts of other men.

The round red headdress, with a blue band, signifies his irresponsibility in his inevitable destruction and that this will take place in the material world, under spiritual influence. The hand holding the yellow rein is not seen, as this force is directed by an intelligent invisible hand, and is not a destructive force without purpose.

The red stirrup shows the support points in the material, that the knight leans on in order to carry out his transformations.

The yellow decorations of the horse have the same meaning as in the Knight of Cups, as well as the points on the breast collar and reins.

The colours of his dress have the same meaning as with the Knights of Cup and Clubs, along with the ground.

UTILITARIAN MEANINGS IN THE THREE PLANES

MENTAL. Representation of everything that intelligence conceives to build in the material; geometric issues, architectural plans.

ANIMISTIC. Affective feelings rooted, stable and progressive.

PHYSICAL. Necessary guidance provided to businesses, which will operate without the need for contingencies, because if someone hinders him, he will hit him with his cane. Good health. Cure assured in cases of serious, long or chronic illness.

INVERTED. No longer able to act, it becomes neutral and no longer has significance.

*

In its elementary sense, the Knight of Coins represents man surrendering to calm, with his mental energies, to build a solid and lasting construct.

REYNE·DEDENIERS

QUEEN OF COINS

SYNTHETIC MEANING

Holding in the left hand a sceptre crowned in a flowery motif, and a coin in the right hand raised high, in profile almost standing, the Queen of Coins, with the crown thrown back on her blue hair, indicates a powerful inner work of an animistic order to ensure, in the best of conditions, the preparation and organization of the exchanges between the individual and his environment.

ANALYTIC MEANING

The crown implies radiance in the universal. Here it is thrown back and is barely visible, if the Queen of Coins is seen from the front, to show that access to the universal is not the aim sought by her, and that her action, according to the meaning of coins, must be directed towards material work. This position of the crown also symbolizes, by its retreat, a psychological and mental condensation, coming from the past, forming the knowledge, that serves as the basis for a favourable manifestation of change. The inner

329

grating and the outer rosettes symbolize means of penetrating into the material.

FEATURES BY ANALOGY

The blue colour of her hair shows that she is clairvoyant and that her conceptions are essentially intuitive. Her dress, of the same colour, reinforces this notion, since she shows her completely enveloped in the psyche.

Her position, half seated and a profile to the left, recalls the activity that characterizes coins, an activity that is necessarily carried out in the interior, since coins are passive. This shows an intimate effort towards a next solution regarding all constructive issues considered by the Queen of Coins, once the preparation for the active work of the Queen of Coins has been completed. The green of back strengthens her support in the physical, and the yellow top rail, her intellectuality.

The sceptre, black as in the coins, recalls the darkness that reigns between the three areas of the coin and that exists in intuition, whose formations always remain secret. The sceptres flowery crown shows the expansion of concentration carried out by the Queen of Coins.

The coin, presented up front, makes manifest the wealth contributed by the queen. It is perched on her fingers and held up high, to show that the action, prepared by her, is ready to be unleashed, as well as her attraction to the higher states, whose relationship with the physical plane, the queen has established.

The belt, which separates the chest from her abdomen, symbolizes a support and a reconciliation between the animistic tendencies and the material tendencies. The 12 points that appear on it, show that she is at the end of the cycle and is oriented towards the universal, and the wide yellow seam, that joins the flesh-coloured belt with the neck of the same colour, shows the divine intelligence illuminating her activity of the psyche.

UTILITARIAN MEANINGS IN THE THREE PLANES

MENTAL. Assurance of success in research, especially those of an abstract order.

ANIMISTIC. Consolation, solid affection, powerful, radiant.

PHYSICAL. Good health; in case of illness, certainty of cure. Affairs in good balance, managed rationally.

INVERTED. Impediments of all kinds, confusion, great difficulty in clearing bad situations, because the means, the queen possesses in acting out materially, obstruct her and trap her in them.

*

In its elementary sense, the Queen of Coins represents the latent and intuitive work of man, which must precede all construction and all changes, in order for them to be carried out in the best of conditions.

KING OF COINS

ROY·DE DENIERS

SYNTHETIC MEANING

Without a crown, with the head covered by a flamboyant hat, that rests on a white headdress, and wearing a rich and diverse costume, the King of Coins, seated, with one leg crossed, the body oriented to the left and the head towards the right, he thus symbolizes mental riches and the sciences of man, which allow, through their judicious use, and depending on the case, the progressive or in the immediate achievements in material constructions, conceived by the mind.

ANALYTIC MEANING

The complexity of the headdress of the King of Coins, indicates the set of working planes, that it embodies and matters on which it reflects. The absence of a crown shows, in effect, that these planes do not radiate in the universal like with the other kings, but that they operate through the means available to man, in other words, by human science, which by themselves cannot provide communication to the universal, the mastery on a higher plane.

FEATURES BY ANALOGY

The triangles in the hat indicate constructions, because the triangle, due to its non-deformable equilibrium, constitutes the essential schematic element of any building[73]. The blue colour of the cap, flesh on the inside and yellow on the outside, indicate deductions and inductions, exerting themselves in vital work, which allow for the directing and the controlling of the material. Its shape as; ∞ determines an effort in a closed circuit, therefore complete and with the possibility of being achieved.

The white headdress, below the hat, is the contribution, rich in knowledge, diverse in currents and with effluence from a higher plane. This denotes in the King of Coins powerful scholarship, diverse and luminous. The white beard, indicating the will and means of execution, confirming an emission of synthetic currents, while the flesh-coloured[74] moustache represents a contribution of nervous force.

The fold on the blue coat, pulled up with the left hand, implies, as a mantle, an envelopment by intuitive forces and, by its removal, a voluntary condensation of the auric fluids, a grouping of activities of the psyche for some specific and precise action. This pulling back, when done

---

[73] This can be seen, observing that the support and frameworks, at the base of every construction, are a set of triangles.

[74] Translator: Please note that he King of Coins in the current Grimaud deck, unlike the card shown, shows a white moustache. Older Grimaud decks have depicted the moustache in flesh colour, however.

on the raised right leg, accentuates the tendency for action and shows that it is imminent.

The numbers 3, 2 and 7, indicated by the 3 black dots on the yellow collar, 2 buttons on the red vest, plus 6 white diamonds and a white line on the black of the armchair in the background, through their shapes, preside over the nature of the operations carried out by the King of Coins in the three planes; mental, animistic and material. On the collar, the 3 dots, or points, indicate abstractions in ternary mode and, consequently, the application of mathematics to the construction of triangles in the hat. The 2 buttons on the vest constitute a polarity, which implies the conciliation of opposites and contain all combinations. The 7 white figures (four surfaces and one line) drawn on the black section of the chair, raised on four legs, show through the number 7 the range of knowledge acquired on the material plane, represented by the double quaternary. Considering these three numbers as a whole, affirms the materialization of the designs from the King of Coins, as the last number is found inscribed outside of him[75]. The 6 black dots on the flesh-coloured seat define the little struggles you encounter in the physical. The 4 black lines that join at the base of the two visible legs of the seat are the small resistances in the processing, and the 5 black lines, above, the small resistances in the transition that leads to the result.

The coin, held by the right hand, therefore active, and leaning on the raised knee, represents the handle of a cranked lever, ready for action. It confirms a forthcoming set in motion and an almost immediate achievement. The coin is small because it represents a compilation of human knowledge, that is, a set of constructions that are more

---

[75] Translator: *"puisque le dernier nombre se trouve inscrit en dehors de luimeme."* Curious comment by Marteau here, perhaps he is referring to the King's pose or part of his dress resembling the number 7 or the quaternary with the number 4?

abstract than concrete. The small size symbolizes the synthesis, which at its biggest potential, is reduced to a single thing.

In this card, the regalness of the figure is not indicated by a crown, since that is absent, but by the richness and diversity of the figures wardrobe, with its multiplicity of elements determines the potency of his strength.

The King of Coins is the only one, who rests on uneven ground. This, because matter is stirred up through your mental activity and material activity. The tufts of grass that sprout from the stirred soil are blooms of intelligence, and the white parts of the soil represent balance and what that brings.

UTILITARIAN MEANINGS IN THE THREE PLANES

MENTAL. Powerful intelligence, universal, perceptive, capacity for introspection in all domains.

ANIMISTIC. Not very spirited, he is neutral in matters of affection. Materialization of hopes, material support.

PHYSICAL. Diverse and very active affairs, changing in nature. Health; fights with an ever-changing temper, since this card is full of fluidic currents. The King of Coins is correlated to Major Arcana II-III and IV.

INVERTED. Extreme disorder, bankruptcy. Complete lack of scruples, imaginations directed towards evil.

*

In its elementary sense, the King of Coins represents mastery in material constructions through science and knowledge.

CONCLUSION ON THE MINOR ARCANA

With the King of Coins, the quadruple quaternary of the figures is completed. Let´s summarize their role:

The four series of Minor Arcana cards represent the elemental and normal game of cosmic forces, from which man can take advantage for his creations. The figures introduced in this book, a side note, manifest themselves through the intervention of the subtle forces of man himself; that is to say, his psyche, his choice of action, according to opportunities, his intuition and his inspirations.

As previously disclosed in the earlier chapters, the Pages correspond to the elemental and subconscious work, which leads to the projection of a desire, and that formulates an expression. The Knights transmit what has just been conceived by the Queens, meaning by man´s intuitive part and that which is born of inspiration, to tune in with the universal; Kings provide the realization.

This realization is made in accordance with four fundamental aspects, that correspond to the four forms of intuition: First; mastery through the will (King of Swords): Second; mastery through work and duty (King of Clubs) Third; mastery through love and mysticism (King of Cups); Fourth; mastery through knowledge and of systems (King of Coins).

TAROT CARD SPREADS

Methods to use in laying out the Tarot in three spreads

1. The reader or interpreter has the obligation to concentrate in order to project himself into the psyche of the querent, as well as in the field of his possibilities in the astral realm. The synchronism of the vibrations of the reader and the client (who must previously have established this alignment), will allow the exploration of the subconscious and the determination of future possibilities.

2. CARD USE IN THE THREE MAIN SPREADS

The reader, after having carefully shuffled his cards, in order to neutralize the vibrations, that may possibly subsist from the preceding consultation, must present them to the client so that he can carry out a shuffling in a circular movement; the reader then consolidates the shuffling of the cards by passing them alternately from one hand to the other. He blows on top from left to right and makes the querent blow as well. These successive operations are intended to ensure the total impregnation of the card stock and to arrange, for a better interpretation, for the reader and the client. It is recommended, according to these different practices, not to cut corners, as this has the consequence of disturbing these vibrations.

3. INITIAL DRAW, DRAW IN A STAR SPREAD OR A CROSS SPREAD

The initial card draw gives the reader the preliminary issue at hand. The first card thus reflects the querent and the card on the left in the subsequent spread. This draw is made with the cards of the Major Arcana only.

After having observed the preliminary draw, the client is asked to think of a number between 1 and 22, at the moment the agreement between the reader and the client has been made, and after their mind is fixed on the question to be resolved, that card is located and put down. This manoeuvre is repeated spontaneously and successively four times, at the request of the reader. The reader takes notice of the number of each card, and then calculates the sum of the numbers that make up of all four cards on the table. The number obtained, if it is higher than 22, must be added up, so that it can be reduced within the limits of 22; the result corresponds to a specific Major Arcana and this will be the central question of the reading. The reader is now in possession of 5 cards (not including the initial card), which must be arranged in the following way:

1. The card to the left, is the querent´s card.
2. The card to the right, represents the outside world.
3. The card above symbolizes the moral or psychological help to the querent.
4. The card below corresponds to the outcome, and
5. The central card reflects the question at hand.

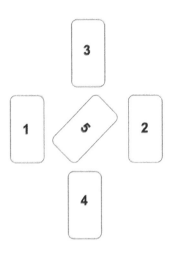

Cross Spread / Star Spread[76]

In order to obtain more accuracy about future events, the sum of the left card and the right card is made, and the number obtained and subsequent Major Arcana allows the reader to conjecture on the obstacles, that will arise in the future. The same operation is executed with the cards above and below and this will indicate the way in which destiny will carry out its outcome. Finally, the sum of the seven cards, now on the table is made, and its results, provides more detail on the answer to the question posed.

4. MEDIUM SPREAD

Always take into account the initial draw as given above. The reader must use the cards of the Major Arcana exclusively for this spread. He will expose the twenty-two cards of the Major Arcana to the client and ask him to choose at random. The chosen cards must be returned to

---

[76] Translator: This spread has several names; Simple Cross, French Cross, 5 card spread, in older Grimaud LWB booklets; Reduced draw and Small draw. However, *Tirage en Croix* has perhaps become the preferred name.

the reader, who takes care not to mix them. He will arrange them one after the other, without reversing their order or presentation. (The Major Arcana must be separated from the Minor Arcana, because the majors represent the principles and the minors reflect the activities that are an extension to those principles).

This 12-card spread is laid out as indicated in the drawing below, placing the first card that comes out in the first position, the second in the second, etc.

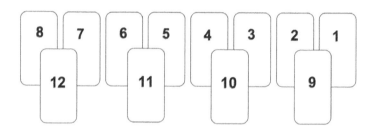

Medium Spread

The reader has before him 12 positions or houses forming a polarized whole, each house is in interaction or in vibration with other houses. This setup has been taken from the Treatise on Geomancy by Eugene Caslant[77] and adapted to the tarot.

The successive correspondences of the different houses that constitute this spread can be interpreted thus:

1st HOUSE – IS THE HOME OF LIFE.
Represents the one who asks the question, or for whom the spread is made, and defines his temperament, character and physiognomy, his complexion, his habits, his ugliness or his beauty, his happiness or his sadness, what he has kept hidden, his intentions, the length or the

[77] *Traite Elementaire de Geomancie* by E. Caslant, Ecole Polytechnique, Libraire Vega, 175, boulevard Saint-Germain, Paris (1935).

shortness of his life. The beginning of all things or in businesses. In what time the business can be started and the success that can be achieved with it.

The head and everything that concerns it: brain, memory, understanding, reason, intelligence, forehead, eyes, eyebrows, nose, teeth, mouth, ears.

2nd HOUSE – IS THE HOME OF ASSETS

It represents the future earnings or personal property of the client, as well as the benefits that he can obtain through his work, by grace or by industry. The honest or unlawful way in which those goods have been acquired. The stability of that wealth and the size of expenses. The benefit that can be obtained from a trip, from a servant, from a friend, from a powerful person. The place where something has been lost or stolen.

The neck.

3rd HOUSE – IS THE HOME OF THE ENVIRONMENT

Represents the brothers, sisters, nephews and other relatives of the client, as well as their relatives and neighbours. His intellectual faculties and his tendencies. The little trips with their little annoyances and satisfactions. Letters and messages.

Shoulders and arms.

4th HOUSE – IS THE HOME OF PATERNAL INHERITANCE

Represents the father and the male grandparents of the consultant, as well as his patrimony, the legitimacy of the son, the longevity of the father. Houses, vines, meadows, gardens, forests with their dependencies, as well as mines, treasures and other stable things. The places where there may be things hidden or kept, such as towers, castles, fortresses, tombs. The city, whatever its size, where the questioner lives, the people who inhabit it, their

fate if it is besieged. The good or bad origin of all things, position disorders, post death reputation, celebrity.
The stomach and chest.

5th HOUSE – IS THE HOME OF YOUR CHILDREN.
Represents the client's children, their number, their traits, their physique. The pleasures and joys of life; banquets, dances, concerts, theatres and all the loves in life, the size and the sex of the child. Speculation, gambling luck, gifts, teaching.
The heart.

6th HOUSE – IS THE HOME OF SERVICE.
It represents the client's illnesses, his servants and his domestic animals, not rideable (lambs, goats, pigs, chickens, etc.), the remedies and the quality of the doctor. The place where the patient is kept, the benefit of having him cared for. Work as a trade. The craftsmen and people of inferior position, the mediators, the false witnesses and bad lawyers. The circumstances relating to the theft of domestic animals. Misfortune, darkness, destitution, shame, fear, and corrupt things.
The belly.

7th HOUSE – IS THE HOME OF THE SPOUSE.
Indicates the possibility of marriage, the character traits of the spouse, the degree of affection or fidelity. Purchases, contracts, processes, discussions; thieves, declared enemies, peace or conflict, and everything that is presented as contrary to the querent. The superiority or inferiority of the adversary in all things; game, duel, company, and in opposition, the value of friendship with another person. The circumstances that accompany weddings.
The pelvis and kidneys.

8th HOUSE – IS THE HOME OF DEATH.

Indicates death or illness of the querent, the brevity or not of its existence, the time of death and the nature of death. The fears and the advantages, it can give you. Inheritances and all things from the dead. The suspicions, the dreams, the drowsiness, and all that ties with the dead. The sadness, toxins, the poisons.

The bladder and genitalia.

9th HOUSE – IS THE HOME OF RELIGION.

Indicates the belief, piety, philosophy, ideals and moral tendencies of the querent. Everything that is related to religion, such as ecclesiastical dignities, the places of worship, a monastery or a hermitage, the different religious services, the clothing of priests and, consequently, ordination, ecclesiastical offices. What pertaining; the philosophical ideas, the conscience, the degree of judgment or madness, the writings, the studies, the functions of an intellectual order to which the client can aspire, as teaching staff and the fame to be reached. What is revered, superstitions, divinatory sciences. The great voyages, their usefulness, their danger and their duration, the fate that will accompany distant expeditions, by land or by sea.

Hips and thighs.

10th HOUSE - IS THE HOME OF THE HONOURS.

Indicates the profession. The dignities, protections, accomplishments of the client, his ambition or his ideals, as well as the favour that can be obtained from these pursuits. Mother and female ancestors. The doctor and his prescriptions (pharmaceutical, drug effectiveness, etc.).

The knees.

11th HOUSE – IS THE HOME OF FRIENDS.

It represents the friends of the querent, the help and benefit that can be obtained from a moral or material point

344

of view, as well as the trust that can be had in them. What can be expected of the one on whom he depends. The support that the butler can obtain from his lord, the assistant from his superior, the children from their father, etc., and, consequently, whether or not he is of good character. The hopes, the value of the promises, the fortune that can be expected in life or in the child, or within a defined period of time, as well as the gifts. The power, wealth or credit of the superior on whom it depends. The advice of the bosses.

The legs.

12th HOUSE – IS THE HOME OF CHALLENGES.
Indicates hidden enemies, their number and strength; the calamities, the riches, the pains of the client, as well as the betrayals that he may fear. What you want to know about traitors, bad servants, thieves and especially what relates to the bad acts, that have been committed. Private but not public enemies, slander. Incurable diseases, ailments, accidents or childbirth. Large animals (oxen, horses, wild beasts, rideable or work animals). The prison. The debts, poverty, misery, the homeless. Exile and its causes, pilgrimages.

The feet.

This Medium Spread, the most widely used, corresponds to man, in his universal role, with all his manifestations.

When the client has chosen his cards, which the reader has arranged, as mentioned previously, he gathers the remaining Major Arcana with the Minor Arcana, shuffling them and purging them again with his breath and that of the client. Then the reader will make the client choose another twelve cards again, which he will place in the same order as the previous. This way the spread will reveal the issue, firstly by means of the Major Arcanum which serves as the basis, the principles that intervene in the different houses or the essential acts that animate these houses, secondly, by means of the second deposited card, the reactions or events to come (whether Minor or Major Arcana).

Depending on the prevalent concern of the client, he can be made to draw additional cards, that will be deposited in the house concerned, in order to obtain additional desired clarifications.

5. HOROSCOPE SPREAD

This spread uses all 78 arcana of the tarot. This complete method provides the total reflection of the client in relation to his role in the universe. Only for the horoscopic spread is the card stock with all the cards shuffled from the beginning. The cards, chosen at random by the querent, are deposited in the twelve positions by the reader, to whom they are delivered one by one, and this successively four times in a row, which makes each house contain four cards. Each of these series of four cards gives the appearance of each of the houses; that is, the reflection of the state in which the client is in, as it relates to that particular house. Each series of twelve with the 4 overlapping cards furthermore correspond to below, where the first drawn card is number 1 and second 2 etc.:

1. To the physical part
2. To the passionate part
3. To the part of the psyche
4. To the mental part

Then 12 cards will be made available to the client, and they will always be deposited from right to left, to obtain the cards house relevance, this will also reveal movements and events that may arise.

346

In short, the first 48 cards will form the static state, the supplementary cards will give the events that will come to pass, 48 + 12 = 60. The remaining 18 cards will have to be used, in step with what details are revealed of each house and assigned to houses of particular interest. It is important, in order to have as accurate a reading as possible, that all the cards are used.

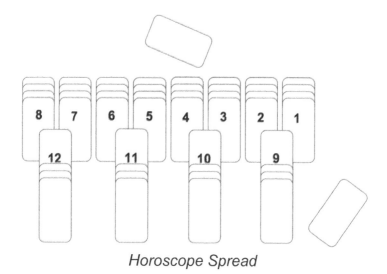

Horoscope Spread

A very important rule to observe is the reaction/interaction of each house to one another. For this, it is essential to understand the meaning of the twelve houses well.

In the interpretation of the cards it is necessary, to do so as thoroughly as possible, to study the situation of the characters expressing their activity or passivity; the colours that intensify a response, through their correspondence with the physical, the psychological or the mental, etc.

The interpreter who is in perfect possession of all these rules for the use of the tarot of Marseille, will be able to give very useful advice and clarifications in full, on the questions that may be asked.

SUMMARY REFERENCE LIST

This summary reference list of meanings, does not appear in the original French version of this book, but it has been added here for easy reference - *Translator.*

JUGGLER In sum, in its elementary sense THE JUGGLER represents man in the presence of nature, with the power to master its currents.

POPESS In sum, in its elementary sense, THE POPESS represents nature, with its mysterious riches, which man must unveil and interpret.

EMPRESS In sum, in its elementary sense, THE EMPRESS represents the fertile power of matter, made available to man for his creations.

EMPEROR In sum, in its elementary sense, THE EMPEROR represents the material energies necessary for man to bestow onto his fleeting creations, in a moment of solidity.

POPE In sum, in its elementary sense, THE POPE represents the obligation, man has to apply divine teachings to his actions and submit to their laws.

LOVER In sum, in its elementary sense THE LOVER represents the sting of desire, which incites man to unite with the universal, whether harmoniously or in a state of imbalance, according to whether he sacrifices himself for it or in the want to derive profit from it.

CHARIOT In short, in its elementary sense, THE CHARIOT represents the dangerous journey of man through the world of the material, to achieve spirituality, through the exercise of his powers and with the mastery of his passions.

JUSTICE In short, in its elementary sense, THE JUSTICE represents the judgment imposed on man by his deep awareness, in order to appreciate the balance and imbalance engendered by his actions, with all their happy and painful consequences.

HERMIT In sum, in its elementary sense, THE HERMIT represents man in his search for truth, calmly and patiently, using logic and light, partly in secret, which he directs with prudence.

WHEEL OF FORTUNE In sum, in its elementary sense, THE WHEEL OF FORTUNE represents man in the midst of present actions, which have their origin in cyclical work of the past and which prepare for those to come in future, on which the divine in the end will award, whatever their vicissitudes.

STRENGTH In sum, in its elementary sense, THE STRENGTH represents the powers available to man, the fruits of his efforts, which he is able to exercise in all planes, when he does so in accordance with divine laws.

HANGED MAN In sum, in its elementary sense, THE HANGED MAN represents, man subverting his action, to orient himself towards the spiritual, in the feeling of hesitation and renunciation.

DEATH In sum, in its elementary sense, Arcanum XIII represents the change of states of consciousness in man, which accompanies the completion of a cycle and is at the beginning of a naturally different type of cycle.

TEMPERANCE In sum, in its elementary sense, TEMPERANCE represents the work of adapting to a new activity, the work of kneading, which man performs in order to readjust to the new, and in a more broader sense, material energies readjusting to spiritual energies.

DEVIL In sum, in its elementary sense THE DEVIL represents a form of human activity, the stirring up of matter, of which man will become a slave, after having achieved a temporary success, or will free himself, with the powers of knowledge, according to weather his goals are selfish or that of material evolution.

TOWER In sum, in its elementary sense, THE TOWER represents the transitory and fruitful constructions of man, always destroyed and always renewed, painful because they ruin ambition, beneficial, because they increase ever the wealth of wisdom.

STAR In short, in its elemental sense, THE STAR represents the celestial light, that makes man glimpse a dawn of peace, hope and beauty, to sustain him in his work, bringing him comforts in his struggles and guiding him through his vicissitudes, and without ever coming short, in his participation of cosmic harmonies.

MOON In short, in its elementary sense, THE MOON represents the chimeric dreams of man, conceived in the dark, under the influence of the agitations of his soul, under the obsessive push of swampy desires, but releasing him from his personal torments, once he is made aware of their pointlessness.

SUN In summary, in its elementary sense, THE SUN represents the light always present in man, manifested in the activity of the day, veiled in meditations at night, which allows him to raise his material, emotional or spiritual constructions in clarity and harmony.

JUDGEMENT In short, in its elementary sense, THE JUDGMENT represents man, awakened from his sleep in the material by his divine aspect, which forces him to examine his soul in all its nakedness, and to judge it.

WORLD In short, in its elementary sense, THE WORLD represents man who is in balance with himself, finding support in the principles of the cosmos in wisdom and spirituality, the generative power and the power of direction. Man, who exercises his power over nature in line with the harmony of the universal laws

FOOL In short, in its elementary sense, THE FOOL represents man, advancing along his path of evolution, without concern and without rest, carrying the weight of his good and bad, he has acquired, stimulated by the ringing of his thoughts, the concerns of the moment or the lower instincts, until the moment in which the balance represented by Arcanum The World is realized.

Ace of Swords In short, in its elementary sense, the Ace of Swords represents the active force, that man displays with firmness and understanding in achieving the triumph of his ideal.

Two of Swords In its elementary sense, the Two of Swords represents the stopping of a specific action, with a view to further enrich this action for a destined maturation.

Three of Swords In its elementary sense, the Three of Swords represents a work of active consciousness deciding on specific actions.

Four of Swords In its elementary sense, the Four of Swords represents joy, the inner ardour of man, created by effort and constructive activity.

Five of Swords In its elementary sense, the Five of Swords represents the decision, that man makes to settle difficulties, that are brought by his crystallization in the world of the elements.

Six of Swords In its elemental sense, the Six of Swords indicates the mental activity of man directed by him to carry out the ordering of and reconciling of material forces.

Seven of Swords In its elementary sense, the Seven of Swords represents the test to which man is obliged to submit himself, in order to become aware of certain knowledge and without which his intimate sense cannot emerge.

Eight of Swords In its elementary sense, the Eight of Swords represents the efforts to liberate man through an inner evolution, a consequence of his mental activities, and which is objectively translated into a reward, granted by destiny.

Nine of Swords In its elementary sense, the Nine of Swords represents for man, the need to carry out persevering work to detach himself from the contingencies, likely to create in him a deceptive stability, which would paralyze his evolution, preventing him from penetrating the intellectual rays into the formation of matter and acquire dominion over them.

Ten of Swords In its elementary sense, the Ten of Swords represents the emotional sense of man, that when clarified by the harmonious balance of his experiences, allows him to act with knowledge of the facts, as well as to involve himself affectionately in the way a mother watches over and protects her creations.

Page of Swords In sum, in its elementary sense, the Page of Swords represents the inner elaboration that occurs in the mind of man, when he is deciding to act.

Knight of Swords In short, in its elementary sense, the Knight of Swords represents the quick command by man, his aptitude for decision making, prior to an unexpected event and that make up destiny unforeseen.

Queen of Swords In its elementary sense, the Queen of Swords represents the obligation for man not to act without having consulted his intuition, awakening through concentration the knowledge of his mental activities about the subject matter at hand.

King of Swords In short, in its elementary sense, the King of Swords represents the achievements of man in all tendencies of his mental activities, when this tendency is accompanied by reflection.

Ace of Cups In its elementary sense, the Ace of Cups represents in man the intimate elaborations of the riches acquired on all levels of the mind.

Two of Cups In short, in its elementary sense, the Two of Cups represents an impetus of material desire, resolving itself in a wide expansion of the soul by feeding its instinctual and egoistic tendencies, leaving knowledge behind to be a source for future evolution.

Three of Cups In its elementary sense, the Three of Cups represents the sublimation of an instinctive receptivity in the riches of superior animism.

Four of Cups In its elementary sense, the Four of Cups represents the reserves that man accumulates through his efforts of the psyche and that are translated for him into a benefit, a quality and as an extension.

Five of Cups In its elementary sense, the Five of Cups represents, on the part of man, the organization of perceptions and sensitivities, extracted from the experiences of the subconscious, in order to gain momentum on a springboard of material feelings and to reach the spiritual plane.

Six of Cups In its elementary sense, the Six of Cups represents the evolution of instinct, feelings and intuition, that man seeks to achieve in order to balance his perceptions.

Seven of Cups In its essence, the Seven of Cups represents man's will to expand. The understanding and realization that is its consequence.

Eight of Cups In its elementary sense, the Eight of Cups represents a visionary proceeding with a balanced and safe judgment, that man, being passive however can only under an appropriate impulse detach himself from.

Nine of Cups In its elementary sense, the Nine of Cups represents the harmonious animistic relationship of man with the world.

Ten of Cups In its elementary sense, the Ten of Cups represents the man who, having accomplished his work, turns to prayer and requests divine help to successfully follow a new path of his evolution.

Page of Cups In short, in its elementary sense, the Page of Cups represents the spiritual and happy contribution, that comes to man, when his evolution of the psyche is accompanied by an offering of the soul.

Knight of Cups In its elementary sense, the Knight of Cups represents the sensitive and affective part of man, susceptible to generous expressions and devotion.

Queen of Cups In its elementary sense, the Queen of Cups represents the feeling of altruism, that man carries deep within, which he can only manifest through the daily efforts of devotion and affection.

King of Cups In its elementary sense, the King of Cups represents the voluntary renunciation of personal will, to confidently open up to the Universal.

Ace of Clubs In short, in its elementary sense, the Ace of Clubs represents the material energy placed in the hands of man to allow him to resist external impacts, or to serve as a lever in helping him construct in the physical.

Two of Clubs In its elementary sense, the Two of Clubs represents an inner potential that is inclined to expand.

Three of Clubs In its elementary sense, the Three of Clubs represents the putting into play of a necessary energy to become aware of man´s instinctual resistance, in order to discipline, coordinate and lean on them in subsequent work.

Four of Clubs In its elementary sense, the Four of Clubs represents the fruitful work of man, reaching his ends through material energy.

Five of Clubs In its elementary sense, the Five of Clubs represents man´s affirmations of free will, not to get stuck in the clumsy energies of the world of the elements and to rise to planes of finer vibrations.

Six of Clubs In its elementary sense, the Six of Clubs represents the efforts of man to discipline his instincts and thus ensure the security of his future.

Seven of Clubs In its elementary sense, the Seven of Clubs represents the possibility of success for man, through effort and active and constant work.

Eight of Clubs In its elementary sense, the Eight of Clubs represents the good conditions, the result of a general equilibrium, that promises man success, if he knows how to overcome the resistance of a stable state, to put his energies back into play.

Nine of Clubs In its elementary sense, the Nine of Clubs represents the man who, takes advantage of the balance, that he has achieved in himself in the management of terrestrial energies, he knows how to determine the right moment of every action, by reflex or by intelligence, depending on what is involved. An immediate decision in time.

Ten of Clubs In its elementary sense, the Ten of Clubs represents the energetic and enlightened will of man, who with tenacity and independence is capable of manifesting the experiences he wants, resulting from the progressive management of his material energies.

Page of Clubs In short, in its elementary sense, the Page of Clubs indicates the fermentation of the material energies available to man and that incite him to act.

Knight of Clubs In short, in its elementary sense, the Knight of Clubs represents the incubation by man of the material energies made available to him, in order for him to manage them at his convenience.

Queen of Clubs In its elementary sense, the Queen of Clubs represents the grouping of intimate forces, that man above all, must achieve to ensure his conquest over material energies and to protect himself from their reactions.

King of Clubs In short, in its elementary sense, the King of Clubs represents the necessity of effort and firm determination in action for success on the material plane.

Ace of Coins In short, in its elementary sense, the Ace of Coins represents man's desire to project onto the environment complex work, made in his image and capable of coming to light by itself for his benefit.

Two of Coins In its elementary sense, the Two of Coins represents an intimate illumination, that ferments the intelligence with a view to future achievements.

Three of Coins In its elementary sense, the Three of Coins represents a mental expansion, that manifests itself through constructive and regenerative work.

Four of Coins In its elementary sense, the Four of Coins represents the inner ideal of man, the conductor of his manifestations in all domains, giving him the power to achieve, whatever his support, in matter or in spirit.

Five of Coins In its elementary sense, the Five of Coins represents man appealing to his active awareness in all domains, applying his building brain to harmonious and balanced activity.

Six of Coins In its elementary sense, the Six of Coins represents the internal improvements, that man makes through an effort to reconcile the currents from above with those from below, in order to balance his alignments.

Seven of Coins In its elementary sense, the Seven of Coins represents man's incitement to action and the decisions he must make, in order to create a steady state for himself.

Eight of Coins In its elementary sense, the Eight of Coins represents man's deductions, comparing what is above with what is below, proceeding from the known to the unknown, receiving in proportion to what he gives, and having to make an equivalent effort in what he wants to get.

Nine of Coins In its elementary sense, the Nine of Coins represents the extensive, altruistic and balanced work of man, with the perspective of his union with the world.

Ten of Coins In its elementary sense, the Ten of Coins represents a harmonious totalization, that allows man to penetrate the depths of things and organize them for the good of others.

Page of Coins In its elementary sense, the Page of Coins presents himself to man, as a messenger, announcing the manifestation of his projects, because he has conceived them in agreement with the high and the low.

Knight of Coins In its elementary sense, the Knight of Coins represents man surrendering to calm, with his mental energies, to build a solid and lasting construct.

Queen of Coins In its elementary sense, the Queen of Coins represents the latent and intuitive work of man, which must precede all construction and all changes, in order for them to be carried out in the best of conditions.

King of Coins In its elementary sense, the King of Coins represents mastery in material constructions through science and knowledge.

Made in the USA
Las Vegas, NV
26 May 2024